Fishkeeping for Kids

Brian Conway

Vital Health Publishing

Fish Facts

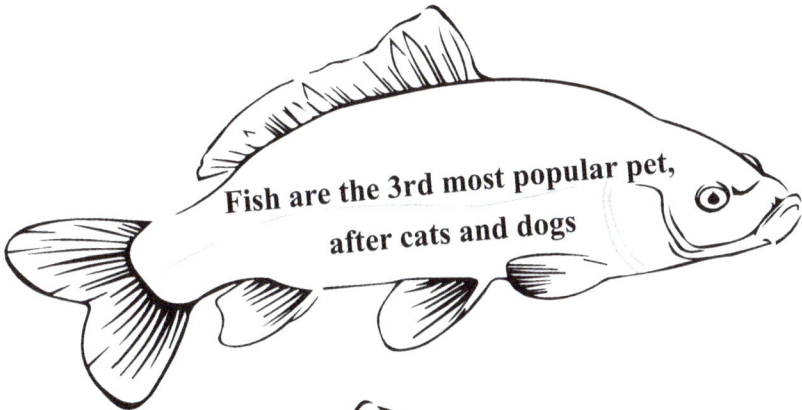

Fish are the 3rd most popular pet, after cats and dogs

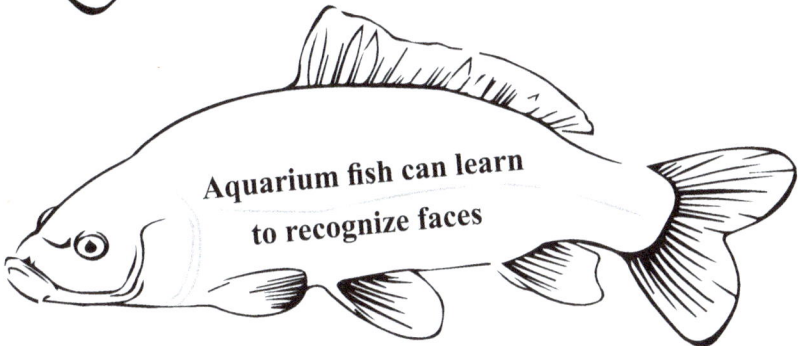

Aquarium fish can learn to recognize faces

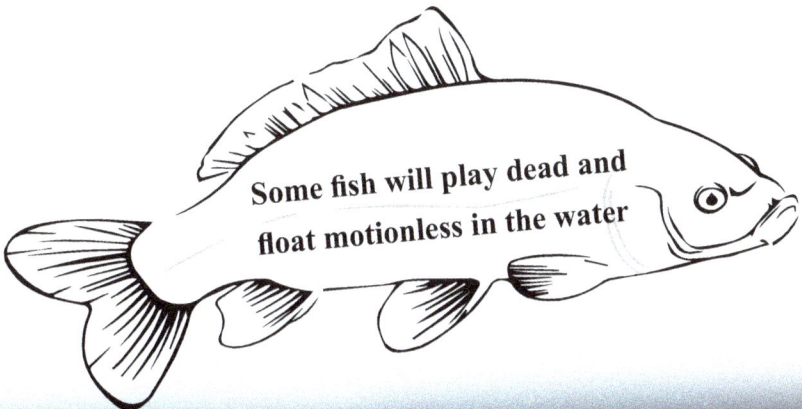

Some fish will play dead and float motionless in the water

Fish Facts

Fish can remember which people give them food

Some fish can change colors based on their environment

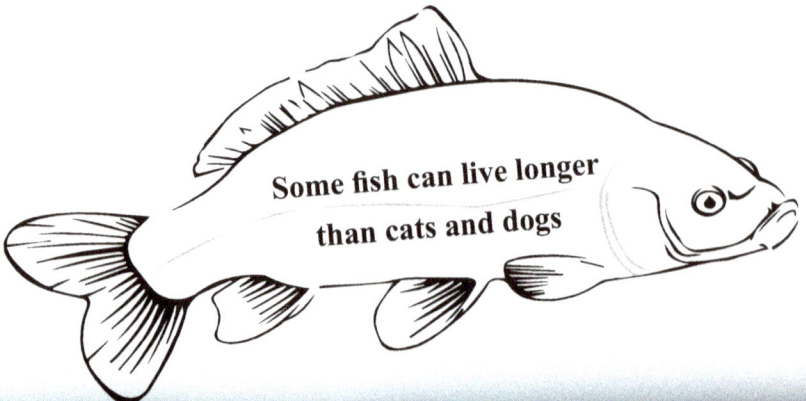

Some fish can live longer than cats and dogs

Published in 2021 by Vital Health Publishing, LLC

Vital Health Publishing, LLC

Hulbert, Oklahoma

Printed in the United States of America

Book Design by Antonio Conway

Visit us on the web at vitalhealthpublishing.com

ISBN: 978-0-9995165-7-7

Table of Contents

Introduction

Fishkeeping for Kids is one of the first fishkeeping books of its kind- a book for kids, from a kid, as well as a comprehensive guide book. This book, even though it is kid-friendly, is for anyone who wants to get into fishkeeping or who just started fishkeeping. You may learn some things even if you are an experienced fishkeeper. This book will teach you everything you need to know to properly care for your fish, as well as some tank design ideas and a basic guide to some common fish. I myself have been keeping fish for over 3 years, and have made sure to clarify everything in this book that I was confused about at first.

I also made sure to avoid things that were especially confusing in the books I was reading when I started, such as complex, hard to keep track of systems for labeling things, like images to describe a fish characteristic with a chart for said images in the front of the book. The book also has an image for every fish mentioned. So let's get started!

Freshwater or Saltwater?

There are two different types of aquariums, and they vary so greatly that they are almost different hobbies. The two are freshwater and saltwater aquariums. Before you start, you need to choose which aquarium type you will have.

SALTWATER AQUARIUM

Saltwater

Most people think that saltwater tanks are prettier than freshwater tanks. Picture a reef crawling with coral, invertebrates and fish in every shape and color imaginable. There are swaying garden eels, jawfish poking their heads out of holes, tangs swooping in and out and an inflated pufferfish. While saltwater tanks are pretty, however, I recommend freshwater because saltwater is so hard to care for. Saltwater is also referred to as marine.

Freshwater

Imagine a beautiful planted underwater jungle. Suddenly, you see a flash of color. You look closer...it's a fish! There are dozens of flashy tetras weaving around the underwater jungle. If you think this slice of nature sounds alluring, then you are in luck. You can have one in your own home! There are many different types of freshwater fish, from tetras to plecos and many in between. In general, freshwater fish are easier to take care of than saltwater fish.

Ultimately, when it comes to freshwater vs. saltwater, there is no right choice. Whichever one you chose, the basic equipment is still mostly the same.

FRESHWATER AQUARIUM

Part 1: Basic Equipment

Chapter 1: Filtration

There are three types of filtration: mechanical, biological and chemical. Mechanical filtration filters out debris in the water. These filters tend to be made of a media such as cotton, foam or, in most cases, a pre-prepared filter cartridge that covers all three types of filtration. Filter cartridges normally have a type of fine media and activated carbon. Biological filtration refers to bacteria that help filter out the ammonia, nitrate and nitrates. Chemical filtration filters out organic material in the water.

Before we go any further, I need to explain the nitrogen cycle. First, fish let out waste. That waste converts to ammonia. Remember that bacteria in biological filtration? Well, it eats the ammonia. That same bacteria lets out nitrites. But there are different bacteria that eat those nitrates and turn them into nitrites. These nitrates are then removed from the tank by plants and water changes. Ammonia is toxic to fish, as is nitrite, which is also toxic in a large quantity. Due to the potential of large measurement spikes, you should not put in fish until your parameters read 0 PPM (parts per million) each of ammonia and nitrate, and five to 20 PPM nitrate, depending on how heavily planted the tank is. Reaching these levels can take from two weeks to four months. Saltwater cycling takes six months to 1.5 years.

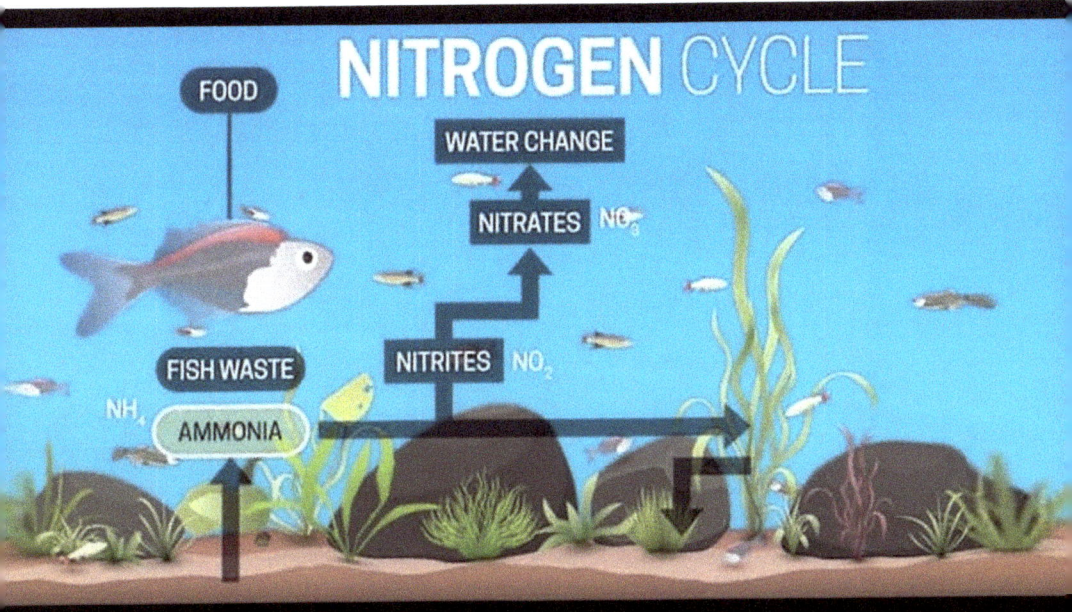

Chemical filtration filters out organic matter, such as dissolved fish food. One type of filter is a "hang on back" (HOB) filter. These work by sucking up water through a tube inserted in the tank. The water flows through the filter, and falls back into the tank. This process works for aeration (putting air in the tank) because when the water flows back into the tank it disturbs the surface, aerating the tank in the process. Sponge filters suck water through a sponge filled with good bacteria and the filtered water flows back into the tank. Sumps tend to only be used for saltwater aquariums. The basic idea for sumps is that the water in the tank flows through a hole in the bottom of the tank, falls into a separate tank below filled with the equipment, such as heaters and filter cartridges, and is then pumped back into the main tank.

HOB FILTER

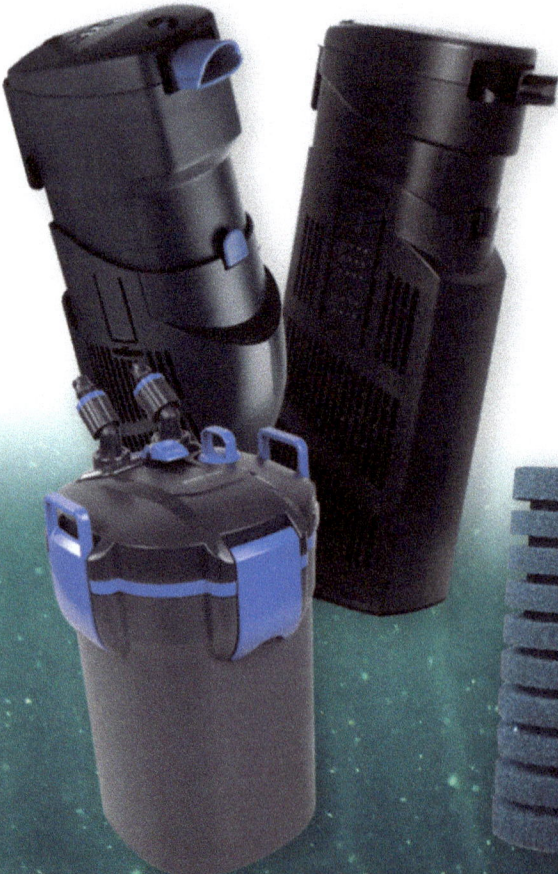

CANISTER FILTERS

SPONGE FILTER

Chapter 2: The Tank

The most obvious thing you need to own a fish tank is… a fish tank! There are two varieties of tanks available. There are glass tanks, which are strong and rigid but also heavy. There are also acrylic tanks. Acrylic is a type of light plastic that scratches easily and can bend under the weight of the water. However, because of its light weight, acrylic is ideal for tanks over 100 gallons. For anything under 100 gallons, glass is best. This is because for 100+ gallons, acrylic is so light that the combined weight of the tank and the water puts less strain on whatever surface it is resting on. In addition, at that larger size, an acrylic tank needs to be framed (have a rubber coating put on the edges to help it stay together). For a tank under 100 gallons, it is better to have a stronger, heavier glass tank.

If you are a beginner, it is best to have a larger tank of 30 gallons or greater, because in a larger tank, the parameters are more stable due to the fish waste being more diluted. You can successfully start with a small tank, as I did with a 10 gallon. The basic parameters include the levels of ammonia, nitrate, nitrite (remember those?) and pH. The pH refers to the acidity or alkalinity of a tank. For the purposes of what I cover here, you won't, for the most part, have to worry about pH, for most fish do fine with the pH of tap water.

Chapter 3: Lighting

All aquariums need light to thrive. As a general rule, use one to two watts per gallon for fish-only tanks, two to five watts per gallon for planted tanks and four to eight watts per gallon for coral. I do not cover much about coral lighting in this book, because a beginner is best off with freshwater (again, saltwater is an option but I strongly recommend against it).

There are three different types of lighting. First is LED lighting. While commonly used in everyday life, there are LEDs meant specifically for aquariums. LEDs have a long life, use less power and put out less heat. However, they tend to be more expensive and they are not the best for live plants. Metal halide lights are perfect for the marine aquarium, they come in a wide array of colors and brightness levels and the light penetrates deep tanks. On the other hand, they do let off a lot of heat. Fluorescent lights are also cheap and are perfect for live plants, but they put out heat and do not last as long as LEDs. Fluorescent lights are tube shaped, compared to the bar-like halides and the lamp-shaped LEDs.

So, what lighting should you use? If you have coral in your aquarium, metal halide is best for you. Fluorescent is good if you have plants and LEDs work best for just fish. If you use metal halide or fluorescent lights, you may need a chiller for your tank, or to get rid of your heater. A chiller is a basic device that lowers the aquarium temperature.

Tube

Metal Halide

LED

Chapter 4: Heaters

Most of the fish in the fishkeeping hobby are tropical, so their tanks require heating. Goldfish are one of the few fish that thrive without heating. Most fish are okay with a temperature of 78° to 80°F. Some heaters are made of a glass tube filled with sand that is heated up. In larger tanks (30+ gallons), you should add two or more heaters. You can also add multiple heaters in small tanks, as long as you are careful not to overheat (for example: in a five-gallon tank, it is better to have two heaters meant for 2.5 gallons than one meant for five gallons). If you have multiple heaters, you won't have as big of a problem if one breaks. It is best to get a heater that measures the tank temperature and adjusts it accordingly. Fish tanks are best not exposed to sunlight, because sunlight causes large algae blooms. Sunlight, as well as artificial light, can heat up a tank. Finally, don't forget to factor room temperature into your calculations.

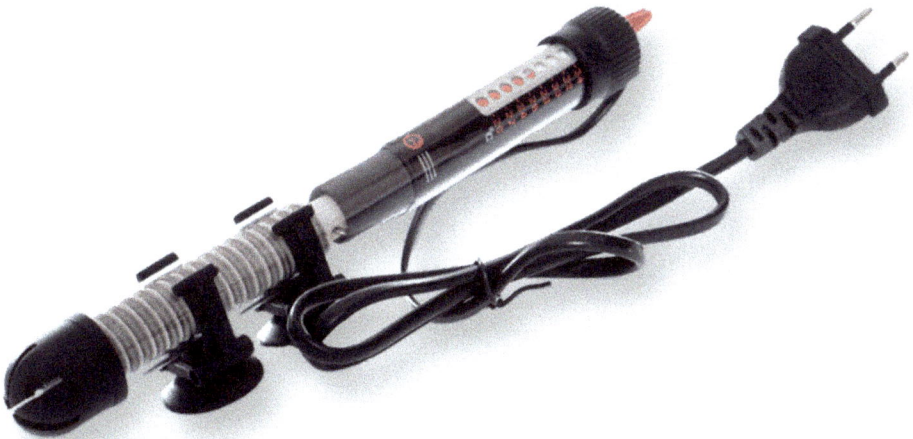

Chapter 5: Aeration and Test Kits

Aeration is necessary for a fish tank. It puts out oxygen into the water, and fish get oxygen from water. Air stones are porous stones connected to a pump. The pump stays outside the water. A long, skinny tube connects the air stone and the pump and the air stone goes in the tank. Some people cut the tube and add a valve that controls the amount of bubbles. Power heads go under the water and pump out water into the tank. Powerheads are measured in GPH (gallons per hour). Other aeration options include wavemakers, which are basically fancy airstones for marine tanks and HOB filters, which pump out water.

AIR STONE

One of the most important things you can do for your tank is test the water. The most reliable way to do this is to use a **test kit**. There are many different types, with varying levels of accuracy. Basic strips that you dip in the water are in general ineffective, and produce results that are wrong. Test kits like API, which I use, are in general more accurate. They are around $20 a kit, and test for all the basic parameters I have mentioned (ammonia, nitrite, nitrate, pH).

The API test kit is easy to use. Basically, you fill a tube with tank water and add a few drops of testing chemicals to it. The water changes color to indicate the levels in the tank. The kit contains a color chart which you can use to compare the color of your sample to come up with the levels. In general, there are a few inaccuracies, but it is accurate enough for the average hobbyist. There are also more expensive, very accurate kits, but for a beginner API is the best to start with. The most important thing to do is follow the instructions your test kit gives you- to the letter.

Often, your local pet store will test your water for free. If the levels are off, they can give you advice about what went wrong and how to fix it. Just be sure to double check what they say.

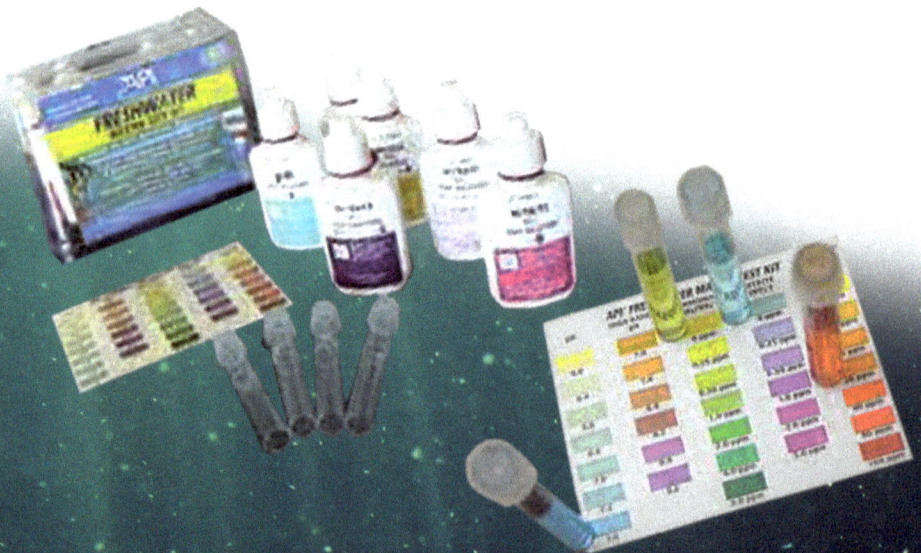

Part 2: Common Aquarium Inhabitants

Chapter 6: Popular Freshwater Fish

You have your aquarium all set up! Now, just one question… what fish will you buy? Tetras are arguably the most popular aquarium fish. Most tetras cost anywhere from $1 to $10. There are many different kinds of tetra to choose from, and in fact my first fish were ember tetras, which prefer softer, more acidic water. They were tiny, at about 0.75 inches. Others, such as congo tetras, can grow to be over three inches. Congos, unlike embers, favor harder, less acidic water. Perhaps the most popular tetras are neon tetras, beautifully patterned with red and blue. Bloodfin tetras are by far the most peaceful tetras I have ever kept. I have a danio, which is prone to being bullied, and not only do the bloodfin tetras get along with the danio, but will actually shoal with them (shoaling is when fish group together, schooling is when fish swim together).

Bloodfin **tetras**, like every other freshwater fish mentioned here, will eat dried food but are best off being alternated between flake and frozen food. Glowlight tetras are mostly a dull white with a vivid stripe of orange. They tend to be on the smaller side of tetras. Cardinal tetras look remarkably similar to neon tetras. The only difference is that the bottom red band on neons stops about halfway, and the rest is the same white as in glowlight tetras. Cardinals have the full red band, and both have a full blue band. Serpae tetras are the same general shades as ember tetras, with black dorsal fins and eye patches near their gills. They are on the larger side as far as tetras go. All of them are fine with temperatures of 76 to 82°F and all of them will survive with normal pH, although congos prefer it a little higher, and embers lower. Congo tetras need a minimum tank size of 30 gallons, and for the rest of the tetras the minimum tank size is 10 gallons.

EMBER TETRA

GLOWLIGHT TETRA

BLOODFIN TETRA

CARDINAL TETRA

NEON TETRA

CONGO TETRA

GUPPIES

Guppies are also up there on the
popularity list. Guppies cost around $3 and grow to one inch in length. They
come in every color variety imaginable. The smallest tank size they should
be kept in is 10 gallons. They are closely related to the less known Endler's
livebearer. The females are more dull in color. To remedy this, some guppy
females have dye injected around their tails, but as a result they become
sterile. Some males have tails almost as big or even bigger than their entire
body!

Oscars are territorial, aggressive, large and one of the smartest fish you'll
find. They are full of personality, from ones that murder everything to ones
that can be kept relatively peaceful in a community tank. However, all oscars
are best off in a tank of their own. These fish are large cichlids (sik-lids),
growing up to 18 inches, so they are best off on their own in a 75-gallon or
larger tank. They normally cost around $20.

OSCAR

SWORDTAIL

PLATIES

MOLLIES

Mollies are brackish water fish. They can adapt to full freshwater and saltwater, but neither is recommended. Platies and swordtails are fully freshwater and are very closely related to mollies and swordtails. Male swordtails have a sword-like extension of the lower part of their tail. All three cost about $3 to $5, and need a minimum tank size of 10 gallons and grow from two to five inches.

Barbs are relatively small (about two inches long), highly active fish that do best in a 20- to 30-gallon tank or larger. Barbs cost anywhere from $2 to $20. Some more placid species can thrive in a 10-gallon tank. One such species is the cherry barb, which I personally have kept in a 10-gallon tank. Cherry barbs only grow to around two inches, while the tiger barb can top three inches. Tiger barbs are extremely active barbs that, when kept in groups of fewer than a dozen, are voracious fin nippers. Because of this, they are best kept in a 30 gallon. You can also get green tiger barbs. Tiger barbs are the most popular of all barbs. The largest barb is the tinfoil barb, growing up to over one foot long! That, along with the fact that barbs are schooling fish,

ROSY BARB

TIGER BARB

GOLDEN DWARF

BARB

CHERRY BARBS

RUBY BARB

TINFOIL BARB

means that tinfoil barbs need a minimum tank size of 120 gallons. Tinfoil barbs need a lot more plant matter than other barbs. Rosy barbs are my personal favorite barbs (shh!), a beautiful rosy red color, with a green hue and a black spot. Golden dwarf barbs are less popular, spotted with gold, white and black. While rosy barbs are my favorite, ruby barbs are the most beautiful by a landslide. They have a dark, charcoal back, tail and upper head, while the stomach and lower head are a beautiful, dark ruby red.

HONEY GOURAMI   PEARL GOURAMI

DWARF GOURAMI   MOONLIGHT GOURAMI

Gourami are perhaps the most popular aquarium fish out there. A few different types are moonlight gourami, pearl gourami, honey gourami and dwarf gourami. Honey and dwarf gourami only grow to two inches, meaning that they can fit in tanks as small as 10 gallons. Honey and dwarf gourami cost only $5 to $10. Pearl and moonlight gourami grow up to six inches, with eight inches for the moonlight. This means that they need a minimum tank size of 30 gallons. They cost $5 to $10.

Betta are another popular aquarium fish. They are kept in tiny tanks that, although they are capable of surviving in, are really too small for any fish. They should have an absolute minimum tank size of 2.5 gallons. They have an organ, the labyrinth organ, that allows them to breathe air. Male betta are extremely aggressive towards each other. Betta are also known as Siamese fighting fish. They come in every color pattern imaginable. Some betta are specially bred to have long, flowing fins. They average a cost of $5 to $10. They grow up to six inches for the

BETTA

giant varieties, although 2.5 inches is more common. Contrary to common belief, you can keep female betta together in some situations. With a large enough (30+ gallons) densely planted tank as well as a separate, permanent home for each betta in case things go south, you can successfully keep a harem (two+ females with a male) or sorority (a group of females) of bettas. One general rule is at least two bettas with a male, for if you have only one female she will be harassed by the male.

KILLIFISH

Killifish are small fish that should be kept in a minimum tank size of five to 30 gallons, depending on the species. Norman's Lampeye Killifish are one of the smallest varieties. When buying killifish, make sure you know if it is annual or not. If it is annual, it will not live longer than one year. This is because in the wild they live in pools. They lay their eggs before the dry season begins and they die while the eggs survive when their pool dries up. The term "Killy" is derived from the Dutch word meaning ditch or channel, not because this fish is a killer in the aquarium. Killifish cost $10 to $25 depending on the species. Killifish are not good community fish, although they do great in species only aquariums

There are many types of **loaches**. One of the largest is the clown loach, growing to one foot long. Clown loaches require a minimum tank size of 120 gallons. Clown loaches cost around $10 to $25. There are also weather loaches, which get more active before a storm. A few other varieties include yo-yo loaches and dwarf chain loaches.

CLOWN LOACH

YOYO LOACH

WEATHER LOACHES

ANGELFISH

There are two types of **angelfish**, freshwater and saltwater; here I discuss freshwater. There is a larger, taller subspecies of angelfish, known as the altum angelfish, that grows up to 10 inches. Unlike their saltwater counterparts, they are fine in tanks as small as 20 gallons, although the tank needs to be high and in that small of a tank they should be kept solitary. Angelfish have the same body shape of a crescent moon and only grow to six inches. They cost from $5 to $20 on average

Apart from plecos, **corydoras** catfish are the most popular catfish. Most varieties cost about $5 to $10, although some can cost more than $50! They are stout fish with downturned mouths, which means they are bottom feeders. They are great companions for messy fish, such as larger gourami, because they clean up the tank. They come in many varieties. Try to avoid dyed corydoras, because the dye quickly fades and the dyeing process is stressful for the fish. Dwarf corydoras require a minimum tank size of 10 gallons, and grow from one to 1.5 inches, and the smallest tank size for normal corydoras, such as bronze cories, is 20 gallons. Normal corydoras grow from two to three inches.

BRONZE CORYDORAS

DWARF CORYDORAS

Chapter 7: Popular Saltwater Fish

Saltwater **angelfish** are truly a sight to behold. For the beginning fishkeeper, the dwarf angelfish are best. Growing no longer than five inches, they are good options for 55 gallons or larger. There are many high quality angelfish frozen preparations, with premium ingredients like sponge and sea urchin flesh. These preparations are perfect for angelfish. The smallest, the pygmy angelfish, is a possible candidate for a tank as small as 30 gallons. They are not as nibbly as some of the larger angelfish. The largest can grow up to two feet long! Larger angelfish, such as rock beauty angelfish, tend to nibble corals and eat invertebrates. The rock beauty angelfish is yellow with a black, triangular body patch. Larger angelfish require a 150 to 300 gallon aquarium. Dwarf angelfish do not eat invertebrates, and tend to nibble at coral less. Some of the most popular dwarf angelfish are flame and coral beauty angelfish. Some of the rarer varieties include potter's, midnight (my favorite), flameback and more. Some larger angelfish significantly change in color as they grow. They can cost anywhere from $20 to $200, with the peppermint angelfish, the rarest, averaging $20,000!

ROCK BEAUTY ANGELFISH

POTTERS ANGELFISH

MIDNIGHT ANGELFISH

CORAL BEAUTY ANGELFISH

FLAMEBACK ANGELFISH

FLAME ANGELFISH

PYGMY ANGELFISH

RED FIREFISH

PURPLE FIREFISH

HELFRICHI FIREFISH

Red **firefish** are one of my favorite fish, with stunning coloration and an unusual dorsal fin. There are also less common purple firefish, as well as helfrichi firefish. Helfrichi firefish are the rarest. All three are members of the dartfish family, along with scissortail dartfish. Normal red cost $10 to $20, purple is $20 to $40 and helfrichi $40 to $50 or even more! All three need a minimum tank size of 10 gallons and grow to 3.5 inches. Like all non-predatory saltwater fish mentioned here (e.g., (lionfish, eels), they are best off when fed alternating flake food and frozen food. `

Tangs are large, active, often beautiful fish. They require a minimum tank size of 80 to 500 gallons (360 for unicorn and similar-sized tangs, at two feet long). Royal tangs, also known as blue and hippo tangs, were made popular by the film character dory in Finding Nemo and Finding Dory. Dory is a blue tang with memory problems. They are herbivores that will devour algae, nori (dried seaweed) and terrestrial vegetables with gusto, although terrestrial vegetables should only be rare treats. Sizes range from six inches to two feet. Perhaps the most common aquarium tang is the yellow tang, at six inches. My favorites are flame fin tomini tangs, with a smoky gray body and flame orange to sun yellow fins. The largest tang, the unicorn tang, looks like something out of a little kid's imagination, with vivid blue coloring and a fleshy horn. Tangs cost anywhere from $20 to $20,000, although $20,000 is very, very, very rare.

FLAMEFIN TANG

BLUE TANG

UNICORN TANG

YELLOW TANG

CHINSTRAP JAWFISH

BLUE DOT JAWFISH

YELLOWHEAD JAWFISH

BLACKCAP JAWFISH

Jawfish dig little burrows in the sand, peeking their head around to look for food. There are four varieties of aquarium jawfish. The most common variety, yellowhead jawfish, need a minimum tank size of 20 gallons, grow to 3.5 inches and have blue bodies and a yellow head that blends in with the sand. Bluedot are brown covered in vivid blue spots,with a minimum tank size of 30 gallons. Chinstrap and black cap jawfish are dark brown and black, with a minimum tank size of 10 gallons. Yellowhead jawfish cost $20 to $30, black cap and chinstrap jawfish from $25 to $40 and bluedot jawfish around $200. Bluedot, chinstrap and black cap jawfish all grow to around two inches.

Gobies might just have the most diversity of any aquarium fish, with freshwater, brackish water and marine gobies. This section is about marine gobies only. Most gobies are $1 - $100. One of the few gobies that costs $100 is the flame goby. One of the smallest common marine aquarium goby, the greenbanded goby at 1.2 inches, can fit in tanks as small as five gallons, and are extremely colourful. The shrimp gobies, such as the yasha shrimp goby, have a symbiotic relationship with certain pistol shrimp. The shrimp dig and share burrows with gobies, where space in the reef is in high demand. The shrimp also help protect the pair with their gun-like claw-snapping that sends out a powerful shockwave. In return, the gobies guide the blind shrimp around the reef and alert them to danger and also help them find food. Shrimp gobies need a minimum tank size of 10 gallons and grow from one to four inches.

GREEN BAND GOBY

SHRIMP GOBY

FLAME GOBY

Clownfish and **damselfish** are in the same family, Pomacentridae. Clownfish are famous for the character Nemo in Finding Nemo. In the wild, damselfish live in groups of thousands, where aggression is spread out evenly. In the home aquarium, they are aggressive, and since they cannot be kept in groups of thousands, aggression is not spread out evenly. For example, take yellow tangs. If you have two, they are constantly picking on each other,

MAROON CLOWNFISH

GREEN CHROMIS

AZURE DAMSELFISH

PERCULA CLOWNFISH

which is unhealthy. However, if you have 12, they will evenly pick on each other. Instead of being picked on half the time, they are being picked on 1/12 of the time. Clownfish come in many colors such as maroon and gold, black and white, black and blue, plain orange, plain white, white with black spots, white with orange spots and many more. Maroon clownfish grow to six inches, large enough to require 30 gallons for a pair and a pair ONLY. Any other clownfish has a minimum tank size of 20 gallons, although they are commonly and successfully kept in five- and 10-gallon tanks; however, I, as a fishkeeper, believe that it is our duty to provide an environment that they can live in comfortably.

Damselfish also come in many colors, such as black with neon blue, blue, green, blue with a yellow tail, black and white and many more. Damselfish grow from two inches, like the blue-green chromis, up to six inches, like the sergeant major. Chromis are a more peaceful variety of damselfish. Damselfish cost $5 to $30, and clownfish $10 to $100, but $100 is usually the price for a matched pair, because it is hard to pair clownfish.

SUNSET ANTHIAS

SUNBURST ANTHIAS

SQUAREBACK ANTHIAS

Anthias are beautiful fish. If you intend to keep a sorority (a group of females), or a harem (two+ females with a male), which are both good options, they require 75 gallons or larger, and they are best kept together, however, one alone can fit in 30 gallons. The most common are fathead, or sunburst, anthias and sunset anthias, but my favorite are squareback anthias. All three tend to cost $10 to $40. Most anthias grow from three to six inches.

Lionfish are well known in the wild, but the smallest varieties are suitable for aquariums, and stay as small as six inches! Lionfish tend to be inactive, staying around the bottom and resting on rocks. They are poisonous, and if stung by one the wounded area should be submerged in water as hot as it can handle. Smaller lionfish, like fuzzy dwarf lionfish, are best in 30-gallon tanks, and larger lionfish, like volitan lionfish, are best in 120 gallons or larger. Lionfish cost around $20 to $50. Lionfish like live food, and will often need to be trained to eat frozen food. For more information on training fish, refer to Part 6, Chapter 30, Feeding.

LIONFISH

MARINE BETTA

Marine betta are nothing like the betta we know of (previously mentioned in this book). They grow to eight inches and are black, and they are completely covered in white spots, including their eyes! They have an eyespot (a spot that looks like an eye) on their tail. They are voracious predators. True of any predatory marine fish, they should not be fed freshwater feeder fish, as this damages their livers. The minimum tank size for marine betta is 55 gallons. They cost $50 to $80.

Pufferfish are well known for their inflating abilities. You **SHOULD NOT** poke a pufferfish just to see it inflate. People do this, and it is very cruel to the fish. Some pufferfish have poisonous spines, and special care must be taken with these pufferfish. Smaller pufferfish, like Valentini Pufferfish, have a minimum of 30 gallons, and larger pufferfish, like porcupine pufferfish at two feet, have a minimum of 300 gallons. Valentini Pufferfish cost $20 to $30 and grow to three inches, and porcupine pufferfish are $40 to $50.

PORCUPINE PUFFERFISH

VALENTINI PUFFERFISH

Chapter 8: Popular Invertebrates

Cherry **shrimp** are the most popular shrimp, hands down. They are a bright cherry red. They are dwarf shrimp and grow to about ¾ to one inch. They can be kept in tanks as small as one gallon, with proper heating, filtration and aeration. This is also true of snowball shrimp and red crystal shrimp. Some people use them as feeder shrimp, feeding them in excess before feeding to fish. This is called "gut packing," and refers to any type of live food. Cherry shrimp cost around $5. As with all inverts except crayfish and panther crabs, they are best fed algae wafers with the occasional treat of fish food.

CHERRY SHRIMP

Snowball shrimp are a bright, snow white. Unlike cherry shrimp, they are not quite so popular, but like cherry shrimp they are dwarf shrimp and grow to ¾ to one inch. Red crystal shrimp also grow around this size. They are for sale in most shops for around $10.

SNOWBALL SHRIMP

RED CRYSTAL SHRIMP

Red crystal shrimp red with shards of white along then. Red crystal shrimp, along with snowball and cherry shrimp, like to eat algae pellets and enjoy high quality fish flakes as a treat. Red crystal, snowball and cherry shrimp all enjoy heavily planted tanks, with plants like Java ferns and Java moss, Amazon swords and moss balls, along with floating plants like duckweed, dwarf water lilies and water lettuce. These shrimp average a cost of $10 and grow to one inch.

Amano shrimp are, gram for gram, the most voracious algae eaters in the shrimp world. Also known as ghost shrimp, they are translucent to the point where you can see their inner organs. They eat fish food and, of course, algae. These are most often used as feeder shrimp. When gut-packed, you can see food inside of them. They need a minimum tank size of 10 gallons, with proper filtration, aeration and heating. They cost around $5 and grow to two inches.

AMANO SHRIMP

PANTHER CRAB

Panther **crabs** are one of the very few freshwater aquarium crabs that live their whole life completely underwater. They are attractively speckled with black and white. These crabs grow up to five inches in diameter, and require 20 or so gallons. They go for around $20 to $25 in most shops. They should not be kept with small fish like ember tetras or dwarf shrimp, for they most likely will be eaten. Small feeder shrimp are an ideal food for them, especially when gut-packed. Panther crabs will accept freeze-dried or frozen foods.

Thai micro crabs cost about $4 to $5 per crab. They are uncommon, and small, with a size of only ½ inch at most. They can be many different colors. Thai micro crabs like marimo moss balls and they like to hang out in the roots of larger floating plants like water lettuce. They should not be kept with anything other than dwarf shrimp (not larger shrimp like bamboo or amano shrimp) and/or fish small like neon or ember tetras. They need a minimum tank size of five gallons. They are scavengers and will eat finely powdered flake food.

THAI MICRO CRAB

WHITE CRAYFISH

Dwarf freshwater lobsters are really just dwarf **crayfish** for aquariums. A 10-gallon tank is suitable for dwarf orange crayfish, while other varieties require 20 to 55 gallons as a minimum tank size. There are blue, orange, red, white, black, gray, brown, purple, green and many more varieties of dwarf crayfish. They will eat anything they can catch, and will be eaten by most pufferfish, excluding pea puffers, which are ½ inch long. Some larger crayfish, such as certain varieties of white crayfish, can grow to one foot long. They require 75 gallons of water to thrive. They cost $4 to $80, with an average cost of $20. I have a four-inch white crayfish in a 20-gallon tank. I alternate feeding with algae tabs, freeze-dried krill and frozen krill. Make sure your tank is tightly sealed so they don't go on a "walkabout."

Snails can be one of the best solutions to algae problems in an aquarium, as they are cheap and efficient. Snails tend to only cost around $2. There are both freshwater and saltwater nerite snails, be sure not to confuse the two. Most snails require around 10 gallons. Be careful when buying mystery snails, as there are many varieties, some growing larger than others.

MYSTERY SNAIL

NERITE SNAIL

PEPPERMINT SHRIMP

Chapter 9: Popular Saltwater Invertebrates

Peppermint **shrimp** look festive, with red and white candy-cane striped coloring. They are very popular, and grow to about two inches long. They average $5 to $10. They are known to help manage glass anemones. They are peaceful and can be kept in groups. As with essentially any other invertebrates, copper and medicines containing copper kill them. They are best off in a 10 gallon tank or larger. Be careful not to confuse them with camel shrimp, which will eat corals. As with all the inverts except lobsters and octopuses, they are scavengers that will eat your fish's leftovers and hardly ever need to be fed. They eat glass anemones, a common saltwater pest.

Brittle **starfish** arms are very skinny, and they are safe to keep with harlequin shrimp, as they are not true starfish. They are good at maintaining algae levels. They grow to 10 inches in diameter. There are many varieties of brittle starfish. Some appear to be spiky, but in reality are hairy. They cost $10 to $15. They should be kept in a minimum tank size of 20 gallons.

BRITTLE STARFISH

EMERALD CRAB

Emerald **crabs** do not grow very large, only to about one inch in diameter. They cost $5 to $10 and can be kept in tanks as small as five gallons. Emerald crabs are nocturnal and will appreciate a cave or rock to hide under. They will also peck at algae.

Tuxedo **urchins** are easy to care for and only get to about three inches in diameter. They are peaceful herbivores, and should not be kept in newer saltwater tanks (under one year old), for they are very sensitive to water parameters. Symptoms include falling off walls, spines falling off and eventually death. They tend to cost around $30 and need a minimum tank size of 30 gallons.

There are a few different types of reef **lobster**, such as the Debelius's Reef Lobster. The most common ones grow to around five inches. The minimum tank size is 30 gallons. They are omnivores. Reef lobsters are highly territorial, so they should be kept only in mated pairs or alone. They cost $20 to $30 and are very colorful

TUXEDO URCHIN

DEBELIUS'S REEF LOBSTER

Arrow **crabs** cost around $20, and tend to grow to around six inches in size, although 10 inches is possible, and females are much smaller than males. Their legs and claws are very long and skinny, with the head only being about one inch in diameter. Their color is red and tan. They look like daddy long leg spiders. It is hardy, and will attack smaller fish and small-to-medium invertebrates. They need a minimum tank size of 30 gallons.

ARROW CRAB

Hermit crabs are one of the best known crabs, and cost $2 to $15. The most expensive common one, the Halloween hermit crab, is orange and red striped. Halloween hermit crabs grow to around one inch. On the cheaper end of the spectrum, scarlet reef hermit crabs only cost around $3. They only get to one inch in size, and have red legs and a contrasting yellow face. All hermit crabs need a minimum tank size of 10 gallons.

HALLOWEEN HERMIT CRAB   SCARLET REEF HERMIT CRAB

CONDY ANEMONE

Sea anemones cost anywhere from $12 to $50. The condy anemone grows to around six inches, and is a favorite of dancing shrimp. Normally in the wild clownfish will live with an anemone, but these anemones are not good for hosting clownfish. They need a minimum tank size of 20 gallons. Condy anemones are semi-aggressive. They will move around and it is best to target feed them (use tongs to place a piece of meat in the center of the anemone) krill or other meaty foods. Do this with all anemones and with a pair of feeding tongs. Condy anemones are arguably one of the best anemones for beginners.

Sea slugs, also known as nudibranchs, cost around $23 and grow to around three inches. Sea slugs, except for lettuce sea slugs, are NOT for beginners, because they are VERY hard to feed and care for. Lettuce sea slugs are a bit of an oddity. They are comical in the way they creep around your aquarium. They need a minimum tank size of 10 gallons. They are easy to care for because they are easy to feed (they eat algae).

LETTUCE SEA SLUG

BUMBLEBEE SNAIL

Bumblebee **snails** won't eat coral, but they are voracious algae eaters and will devour dead creatures. They are yellow and black striped like a, you guessed it, bumblebee. They can get the slime out of the tiny corners, and are very quick for snails. Their max size is ½ inch, and they cost $3 to $5. They are easy to care for and peaceful with a minimum tank size of five gallons.

Not to be confused with freshwater nerite snails, marine nerite snails have a maximum size of one inch, and cost $3. Nerite snails will lay numerous eggs which appear as spots on the glass. Like all other marine snails, care must be taken to make sure that hermit crabs don't kill your snails for their shells. They need a minimum tank size of 10 gallons.

The Margarita snail is one of the most sought-after home reef inhabitants. This is because they can consume large amounts of algae, including nuisance hair varieties. Plus, unlike some snails, Margarita snails are cheap and peaceful towards corals, invertebrates and other tank mates. Also known as the Little Margarite, Pearl or Pearly Topped Snail and Stomatella Limpet, the Margarita snail has a brown body and a smooth shell, and may grow up to one inch as an adult. They cost $2 and need a minimum tank size of 10 gallons.

MARGARITA SNAIL

MARINE NERITE SNAIL

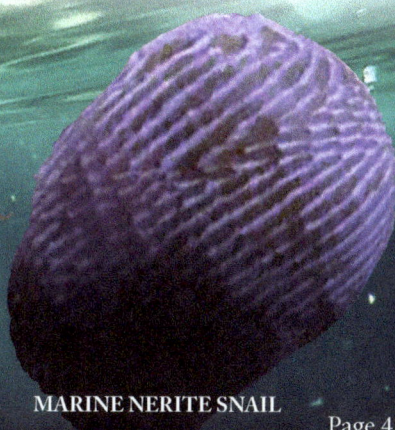

Chapter 10: Large Creatures

Bala "**sharks**" are really just freshwater catfish. The term freshwater shark was a marketing idea because, after all, who doesn't want to own a shark? These are large, powerful fish, growing to over a foot long and being able to jump six feet out of an aquarium, and they won't survive the fall, so therefore special care must be taken when cleaning a tank. They cost around $3.50 and need a minimum tank size of 150 gallons. They aren't particularly picky with the food that they eat. They are likely to eat whatever they can fit in their mouths.

BALA SHARK

Goldfish. Classic goldfish. No, not the kind you eat, the living variety! Maybe one of the most iconic fish of the hobby, most people know what these are. Goldfish are a popular pond and aquarium fish alike, although they are coldwater fish. In a pond, well, I don't think ponds get smaller than 20 gallons, which is the minimum aquarium size for goldfish. Goldfish are, in my mind, without a doubt, the most commonly abused fish in the fishkeeping hobby. These fish grow to one foot long, and when they "grow to fit the tank" goldfish are being stunted. While their body can't grow, their organs do, and kill them. Goldfish naturally live for years, not days. The rule for goldfish is 20 gallons for one and an additional 10 gallons for each additional goldfish. For example, you can have four goldfish in a 55 gallon tank. They cost $5 to $50 and will eat almost anything.

GOLDFISH

PLECO

Plecos, also known as plecs, are commonly kept in tanks as small as 10 gallons, when they grow up to two feet and have a minimum tank size of 150 gallons. They grow from 1½ to two feet long, and if you buy them young, at about one inch long, they cost only $5 - $10. However, if you buy them fully grown, they cost from $30 - $50. The same rule applies as with goldfish as compared to the "grow to fit the tank" myth. They have the same feeding requirements as tangs.

Knifefish are fascinating creatures, truly living up to their name. These are huge fish, the smallest just under a foot and the largest over three feet! Knifefish cost anywhere from $20 to $80. The smallest knifefish, the zebra macana knifefish, has a minimum tank size of 55 gallons. The most common (and probably the prettiest), the black ghost knifefish, grows to 1.5 feet and has a minimum tank size of 180 gallons. They are carnivores and should be fed meaty or live foods.

BLACK GHOST KNIFEFISH

ZEBRA MACANA KNIFEFISH

CLOWN KNIFEFISH

APPLE SNAIL

Apple **snails** are not for small aquariums, for the name is a bit too literal. Apple snails are called so because they grow to the size of apples! They need a minimum tank size of 10 gallons for juveniles and 30 gallons for adults. They are scavengers and grow to six inches. In fact, they are the largest freshwater aquatic snail.

Groupers grow from two to eight feet, the smallest (and, in my opinion, the handsomest) grouper is the panther grouper, with a minimum tank size of 120 gallons. It is white with black spots. Groupers will eat any large, meaty foods, but I would recommend feeding them silversides (a marine fish) every day, with a live feeder goldfish every week. They cost $25 to $200.

PANTHER GROUPER

Chapter 11: Plants

Java **ferns** are one of the most popular beginner plants. In fact, my first live plant was a Java fern. They can tolerate hard water and high pH, and even brackish water. Java ferns grow best on driftwood. Do not release them, or any other plant, into local bodies of water, for they are so hardy. While not invasive yet, (to my knowledge) this is something I could easily imagine happening. Most herbivores dislike the taste of Java ferns, but Java ferns are rumored to be poisonous to fish (of course, that's a myth). Java ferns cost $5 to $10.

JAVA FERN

Java **moss**, another good beginner's plant, is both easy to care for and thrives in low lighting. Java moss needs something to grow onto, compared to Java ferns. Java moss may require trimming. It costs $12 for a five-inch bamboo stick covered in Java moss at LiveAquaria (an online aquarium store)

JAVA MOSS

Amazon sword plants are background plants, compared to Java ferns and moss, which are mid-ground plants. There are also foreground plants. Amazon sword plants enjoy moderate lighting. They make a great focal point when used individually. They cost $5 to $10.

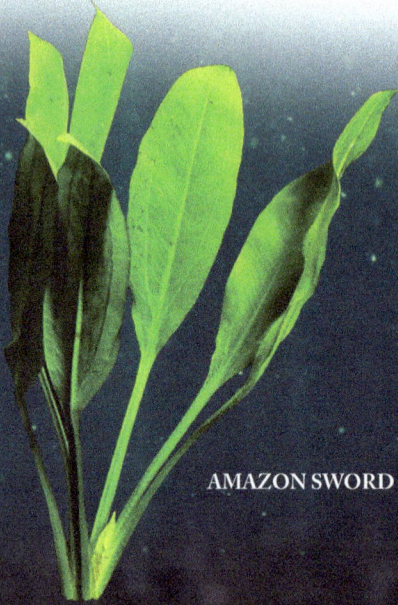

AMAZON SWORD PLANT

The smallest common **dwarf water lily**, chrysantha, is a pond plant, as are most dwarf water lilies. They grow up to three feet in diameter, and cost around $25. They are commonly sold at around the size of one foot. They have striking, cup-shaped blooms.

CHRYSANTHA BLOOM

Banana plants are foreground plants, going at the front of the tank, and cost $2 to $5. They have banana-like roots that store nutrients. They can have a problem with floating until they start sending out new shoots. They like moderate light and do best, like with all plants, with an aquarium fertilizer. Banana plants are amphibious and can grow partially or fully submerged.

BANANA PLANT

Anubias plants like moderate lighting. They grow to be around eight inches and cost $5 to $10. It is a hardy plant but must have a decent light source as well as a substrate to grow in. It can be attached to wood and grows well from cuttings. The photo is of anubias nana.

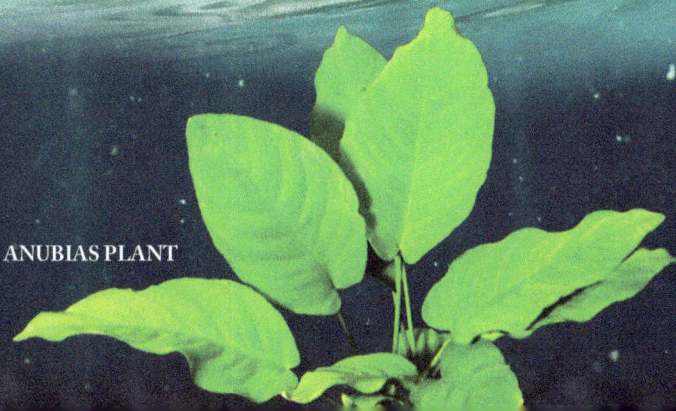

ANUBIAS PLANT

Water wisteria, also known as wisteria, is one of the best beginner plants. It is also a good choice for a tank used to breed livebearers. It costs around $7, and grows to over 1.5 feet. Water wisteria likes moderate lighting, at least two to three watts per gallon.

WATER WISTERIA

Moss balls are often faked with clumps of Java moss tied into a ball. Make sure that your moss ball is actually a moss ball by lightly picking at it. Java moss gives out easily, whereas moss balls are more resistant. Moss balls tend to cost $5 to $10. Moss balls like moderate to high light, with the perfect median being three watts per gallon. Shrimp love moss balls, and occasionally fish will "play" with it and bump it around.

MARIMO MOSS BALLS

JAVA MOSS

Chapter 12: Creatures to Avoid

Mandarin fish, especially green mandarins, can be very hard to care for. While green mandarin fish only grow to around three inches (and cost $30), they need a minimum tank size of 55 gallons. Why, you may ask? Because mandarin fish require small live copepods (like sand fleas) that are found in live sand. To determine if your tank is ready, take out a decoration and put it in freshwater. If you see sand fleas, your tank is ready for a mandarin fish. They are worth the effort, with a dark orange body with dark teal hieroglyph-like markings, and a vivid orange-and-blue striped tail, tipped with bright blue. They can live with other fish, but choose calm, peaceful fish like firefish.

GREEN MANDARIN

ATLANTIC PYGMY OCTOPUS

Octopuses are very smart, so in my opinion they should not be kept in aquariums. But if you want to try keeping one, keep in mind that these are very demanding creatures. The Atlantic pygmy octopus, also known as the dwarf octopus, is NOT a creature for beginners, nor are any other octopuses. They are delicate, as are all octopuses. The dwarf octopus can be surprisingly strong, so in the home aquarium, it is best to anchor the rocks, or even glue them together to keep the octopus from toppling the rocks into the glass or onto itself. Always approach the octopus slowly to avoid causing it to release its ink cloud in defense. In the aquarium, this release of ink will require a large water change to avoid its death. They should be fed shell-on frozen clams. They grow from six to eight inches, need a minimum tank size of 55 gallons and cost $60 to $80

As I mentioned earlier, **sea cucumbers** are NOT for beginners, for they are very sensitive to the water parameters. They average a cost of $25, and can grow from three inches to one foot long. With its brown body spotted with white and dressed in numerous white spines, the tiger tail sea cucumber is also a visually stunning addition to the home aquarium. Since it is a very adept and agile scavenger, the Tiger tail sea cucumber can clean gunk from beneath rockwork and tight corners. Tiger tail sea cucumbers grow to around one foot long and need a minimum tank size of 80 gallons. Sea cucumbers need a minimum tank size of 30 gallons for the smallest, the spiny sea cucumber.

TIGER TAIL SEA CUCUMBER

SPINY SEA CUCUMBER

Butterflyfish are, in my opinion, the prettiest fish in the ocean. Perhaps one of the best species, Indian vagabond butterflyfish, stays small, and is easy to care for, for butterflyfish. Butterflyfish have very low survival rates, are very sensitive to water parameters, only eat live foods (if they eat at all), and die within 2 weeks of being bought over 80% of the time. They cost from $20-$150, and have a minimum tank size of 55 gallons to 180 gallons.

INDIAN VAGABOND BUTTERFLYFISH

While **eels** are a cool fish, they are definitely one to avoid. With the exception of a few rare, expensive eels, an eel will grow as thick as a baseball bat and almost two feet long. They also are slightly blind and target food by smell- meaning most fish aren't safe with them. They cost $20-$800.

SNOWFLAKE EEL

BLUE STRIPE PIPEFISH

BANDED PIPEFISH

Pipefish ARE NOT for the beginning aquarist because they are very delicate. They are peaceful fish and must be kept with like-minded fish. They are stronger swimmers than seahorses and cost $25 to $50. My personal favorite, the banded pipefish, is at the higher end of the price spectrum. Banded pipefish grow to seven inches and need a minimum tank size of 55 gallons. Another pipefish, the bluestripe pipefish, is the smallest of pipefish with a max size of three inches and a minimum tank size of 30 gallons. They eat mysis shrimp.

Everybody loves **seahorses**! These lovable creatures have been made easier to keep due to captive breeding programs. They are trained to eat frozen mysis shrimp. However, these creatures require an expert touch. They are VERY delicate and in the wild eat all day long in small amounts. Therefore, they need to be fed as little and as often as possible in the home aquarium. Seahorses cost $100. Seahorses come in many colors. The most common are yellow, orange and black. The smallest of the seahorse clan, the dwarf seahorse, only grows to about two inches, and a pair can be kept in a five-gallon tank. A good general rule for seahorses is to have the tank at least three times as tall as the seahorse's max size, which for some seahorses is 10 inches. It's hard to have a solid minimum tank size for seahorses, for example more seahorses could be kept in a 30-gallon "high" than a 30-gallon "wide."

DWARF SEAHORSE

CAMEL SHRIMP

Camel shrimp are pretty, live in groups, are easy to care for and peaceful. So why are they not for beginners? Because they tend to eat corals. Camel shrimp are best kept in groups of three to five. They cost around $10, grow to two inches and are scavengers, eating most any food and need a minimum tank size of five gallons for one or 10 gallons for a group, which is preferable.

Another reason to avoid certain creatures when starting out are that fish can be incredibly expensive. Two of the most expensive fish are the **peppermint angelfish** and the **platinum arowana**. The peppermint angelfish costs $20,000 to $30,000. It is not the best fish for beginners, compared to, say, a $5 hardy green chromis. They are red with stripes of white. The platinum arowana makes peppermint angelfish seem like something from a dollar store, with a whopping $200,000 - $300,000 price tag. These are the most expensive fish in the world, which is surprising because usually saltwater fish cost more. They are hard to breed and are actually a mutant variety of arowana, adding to that insane price tag. They need a minimum tank size of 300 gallons, enjoy live crickets and grow from two to three feet.

PEPPERMINT ANGELFISH

PLATINUM AROWANA

Harlequin shrimp are, without a doubt, the most beautiful and demanding shrimp. Not exactly cheap, they cost $25 to $50. They feed on live starfish and sometimes sea urchins, although there have been reports of them eating brine shrimp. They will eat the tube feet of the starfish. They should be fed a live starfish every month. Harlequin shrimp do have a bit of a dark side, they will force feed a starfish to keep it alive only to eat it again. Harlequin shrimp have shield-like adaptations, used to flip starfish over. They are inquisitive creatures that grow to only 1.5 inches and need a minimum tank size of five gallons.

HARLEQUIN SHRIMP

Part 3: Selecting and Buying Fish

Chapter 13: Finding A Fish Store

I was lucky enough to have a good local independent fish store when I first started out. When choosing your store(s), there are a few standards that need to be met before making any purchases, however. First off, is the staff knowledgeable? Can you ask to buy an oscar and a neon tetra for a 10-gallon tank and have them tell you what a dumb idea that is, or warn you that the tetra needs companions and the oscar needs a larger tank? If you ask them something they don't know, do they have books that they will flip through until they can answer your question? Do their fish look healthy? Are their tanks clean? If more than one of these questions gives you an answer of "no," you should look elsewhere for buying supplies.

Another option for buying fish is to do it online. There are many good sites out there, and they send you fish in the mail, which is a cool experience, and the prices tend to be cheaper than buying local. You do have to pay relatively expensive shipping most of the time, however. One of the main disadvantages with the online option is that you cannot see what you are buying beforehand. However, many sites have a "what you see is what you get" (WYSIWYG) section. WYSIWYG is more expensive, although there may be more exotic specimens than what is available for sale in the other areas of the shop.

FLIP
AQUATICS
SETTING THE STANDARD

Chapter 14: What Fish to Get

First things first, when buying fish, you must make sure you know the minimum tank size of the fish you want to get. Just because your LFS (local fish store) has that cute little two-inch pictus catfish in a 10-gallon tank doesn't mean you should buy it for a 10-gallon tank . In this case, you should buy it for a 55-gallon (or larger) tank, because that cute little two-inch pictus catfish grows into an eight-inch active scavenger. The general rule for stocking is one inch per gallon, but this only works with slender-bodied fish. For example, an eight-inch stick catfish is slender and has way less bioload than a chunky eight-inch oscar. And you cannot keep that chunky eight-inch oscar in a 10-gallon tank. A good rule for determining what fish will fit in what tank is to take your tank size divided by five and that equals the max size of a fish you can keep. For example, in a 30-gallon tank, you could keep a six-inch moonlight gourami.

NEVER buy a fish because it's cool or cute or something along those lines. This is a recipe for disaster. If you have a five-gallon tank and you buy an ornate bichir because it looks cool, you will later find out it grows to two feet and has a minimum tank size of 180 gallons, which you can't afford. If that's not a worse-case scenario, I don't know what is.

This book features only a freshwater compatibility chart, for as a beginner I hope you aren't going to be doing saltwater. There are exceptions, of course. One example is plecos and cichlids getting along. However, a two-inch clown pleco with a 15-inch oscar spells disaster. This guide is simple: green means in most cases they will be fine. Yellow means proceed with caution and red means that in most cases they won't get along.

Freshwater Compatibility Chart

	Plants	Loaches	Danios	Catfish	Cichlids	Killifish	Plecos	Barbs	Tetras	Gourami	Betta
Betta	Green	Green	Green	Green	Red	Yellow	Green	Red	Green	Green	Green
Gourami	Green	Green	Green	Green	Red	Green	Green	Red	Yellow	Green	Green
Tetras	Green	Green	Green	Green	Red	Green	Green	Green	Green	Yellow	Green
Barbs	Green	Green	Green	Green	Red	Red	Green	Green	Green	Red	Red
Plecos	Green	Green	Green	Green	Green	Green	Green	Green	Green	Green	Green
Killifish	Green	Green	Green	Green	Red	Green	Green	Red	Green	Green	Yellow
Cichlids	Red	Yellow	Red	Green	Green	Red	Green	Red	Red	Red	Red
Catfish	Green	Green	Green	Green	Green	Green	Green	Green	Green	Green	Green
Danios	Green	Green	Green	Green	Red	Green	Green	Green	Green	Green	Green
Loaches	Green	Green	Green	Green	Yellow	Green	Green	Green	Green	Green	Green
Plants	Green	Green	Green	Green	Red	Green	Green	Green	Green	Green	Green

Key:

- Red — Not Compatible
- Yellow — May Be Compatible
- Green — Are Compatible

Chapter 15: Buying Livestock

It's time to buy your first fish!

There are some guidelines to follow before taking the plunge. If you are buying online, buying a fish is as simple as adding to cart and clicking "purchase." If buying from a WYSIWYG (what you see is what you get), select your favorite(s) of the available fish. Make sure that you do your research on your fish. Also be sure to confirm that the fish is/are healthy, using these questions as a guide:

- Are its eyes cloudy?

- Are its fins ripped?

- Is it bloated with scales sticking out?

- Is it showing odd behavior (swimming sideways, hiding more than is normal for the species, etc.)?

- Is it missing scales (if the species is one with scales)?

- Ask the dealer to feed the fish before purchasing it. Is it refusing to eat?

- Is its belly skinny (more than usual for the species)?

- Are the bases of the fins reddish-pink (if unusual for the species)?

- Are there dead fish in the tank with it?

These questions must also be asked about ALL of its tank mates. If the answer is "yes" to ANY of these questions about ANY fish in the tank, do not buy the fish, for it is probably sick. If the answer is "yes" to one or more of these questions, it also might mean they are stressed.

SICK FISH

Watch as the dealer nets and bags the fish. This will also help you determine the quality of your LFS (local fish store). Keep these key questions in mind as you watch:

- Is the dealer chasing the fish with the net, or is he/she guiding the fish into the net? The ideal situation is when the dealer is trying to guide the fish into the net.

- Is the dealer patient, and will he/she try to get the fish you want out of a crowd? The answer to this should also be "yes."

- Finally, is the dealer loading the bag with anti-stress medication from a bottle? There is no right answer to this question, as this is a matter of personal preference. The medication is helpful to the fish, but can be harmful in the display tank. If you will be introducing the fish into a tank with inverts, make sure the medication does not contain copper, which is toxic to invertebrates.

Buying plants is relatively simple. If the answer is yes to any of the following questions, don't buy the plant. Are the leaves falling off? Are the leaves unnaturally brown? Make sure the plant stays small enough for your tank. For example, you don't want to buy a Madagascar lace plant to find out it is hard to care for and, under the right conditions, grows to over two feet tall.

SICK AQUATIC PLANT

Chapter 16: Acclimating Fish

For freshwater tanks, acclimation should be from 40 minutes to one hour in the plastic bag you bought them in. Acclimate them into the quarantine tank first, and then once you are sure they are disease-free, you can acclimate them in a sandwich bag into the main tank.

Here are a few tips to make the journey to a new home more enjoyable for your fish: First, you should always add new fish at a rate of least two at a time. This minimizes the chances of one fish being picked on a lot. Second, you should always put your new fish in a quarantine tank for the first couple weeks. Third, the final thing to do before moving it to the display tank is feeding the already existing fish. This helps reduce aggression. You should also rearrange your tank decorations. This helps distract the existing fish and breaks up territories, again, reducing aggression. You could also pick up a few new decorations. That way, none of the fish are familiar with the decorations, giving new fish a chance to claim it. Go for at least one day (two for shy fish, like gourami) fasting the new fish (it can live without the food). This gives it time to settle in before it has to compete for food.

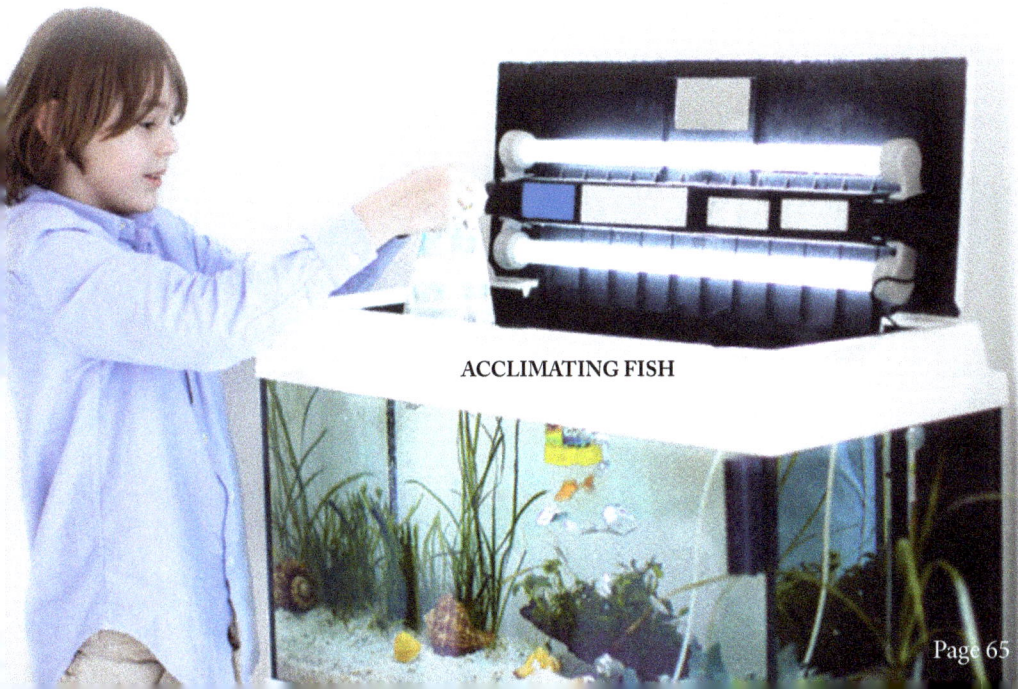

ACCLIMATING FISH

It's time! After all the research, checking and double checking compatibility and minimum tank size, quarantining your fish for three weeks to make sure they are parasite-free, it's time to release them. I do NOT recommend using a net to move the fish from the quarantine tank to the main display tank. Instead, use your water change bucket and MAYBE a net to guide the fish into the bucket. Then, lower the bucket into your main tank and let the fish swim out on their own. This approach minimizes both stress and air contact. This method and the one mentioned above are just two ways of releasing fish, and they both will work.

Finally, the fish is in the main tank! This is the climax of the adventure of fish tanks… until you decide to add more fish or even get another fish tank. When the fish is in the tank, you need to observe it. If it's being bullied, you must decide whether you want to put the bully in quarantine, return the bully or return the new fish. It is normal for your fish to hide more often than usual in the first couple of weeks. Again, do more research on ANYTHING you don't know about your fish.

Part 4: Basic Diseases

Chapter 17: Types of Diseases

Most of the time, if you keep the tank clean and healthy, its inhabitants will not get sick. Fish can get sick if they are stressed out or in an unhealthy environment.

Fish diseases

Illustrated here are some of the more common ailments that befall fishes in the aquarium. Some are due to parasites introduced into the aquarium with live foods or plants from other waters; others are bacterial infections brought about by poor aquarium hygiene and lack of maintenance.

Tailrot/Finrot

These very obvious symptoms appear on fishes of poor health. Low temperatures, physical damage, and unhygienic conditions in the aquarium all encourage the harmful bacterial action.

White spot

Tiny white spots cover the fins and body. A tiny parasitic ailment that some aquarists believe lies dormant in every fish aquarium waiting to attack weak fishes.

Velvet disease

Infected fishes have a cloudy appearance. Caused by a parasite *Oodinium*, which goes into an encystment stage. Will respond well to widely available proprietary cures.

Skin flukes

The *Gyrodactylus* parasites burrow into the fish's skin and stay near the surface. Affected fishes lose color and become feeble. Responds well to treatments.

Eye infections

Cloudy eyes (below) are often due to fungus or a worm cataract, Proalaria. Protruding eyes (main illustration) usually suggest that other diseases are present as well.

Mouth fungus

The slime bacterium *Chrondococcus* causes this. It is unrelated to body fungus.

Lymphocystis

These very obvious symptoms appear on fishes of poor health. Low temperatures, physical damage, and unhygienic conditions in the aquarium all encourage the harmful bacterial action.

Fungus

Fungus (*Saprolegnia*) attacks fishes already weakened by phisical damage, parasites, or poor conditions. Also liable to affect fishes if they are transferred to widely differing aquarium waters.

Pox

White spots join to form large patches. Affected fishes become emaciated and are often left twisted. Faulty diet and lack of vitamins are likely causes. May heal itself under healthy aquarium conditions.

Slimy Skin

Fishes afflicted with this condition develop a thin grey film over the body. The parasites *Cyclochaeta* and *Costia* (shown at above left, right) cause the fish to produce excessive amounts of slime.

Dropsy

The scales protrude noticeably due to an accumulated liquid in the body. The fluid from infected fish may infect others. To prevent this happening remove any sick fishes from the aquarium promptly.

Gill Flukes

The flatworm *Dactylogyrus* attaches itself to the delicate gill membranes and causes an extremely obvious inflammation. Infected fishes develop an increasing respiration rate and gaping gills.

Ich, also referred to as white spot disease, is arguably the most common aquarium disease. It is a parasite that presents as little white spots on the fish. There is also a marine version of this disease, which is almost the same, except that it occurs in marine fish.

Popeye is another parasite that causes the eyes of a fish to pop out, though the eyes do not actually fall out of the socket. I once had a pearl gourami that got infected, and it died. (I suspect the death occurred because my dwarf gourami broke its spine, but the popeye didn't help.)

Although **fighting** is not technically a disease, fish fighting can be as deadly, or even more so. Even if the losing fish is not injured, the stress can contribute to fish getting diseases (if they fight enough).

Fin rot eats away at the fins. The difference between fin rot and a fish ripping the fins off another fish (happened to a betta of mine) is that fin rot is related to a bacteria. The visual difference is that if a fish has fin rot, the base of the infected fin will appear pinkish-red.

Dropsy causes a fish's stomach area to swell up. The scales stick out as well. Dropsy is particularly easy to see and identify.

Hole-in-head disease eats away at a fish's head, leaving multiple holes in a fish's head. While this sounds gruesome, It is really an easy disease to treat. All you need is the right medication.

Swim bladder disorder causes a fish to lose control of its ability to control its swimming. A fish with swim bladder disorder may swim sideways or upside down, and may not be able to control what level of the tank it stays on.

Chapter 18: Quarantine Tanks

Sometimes, when a fish gets sick, leaving it in the main tank will infect everything. This is where quarantine tanks come in. They are smaller, basic "hospital tanks" for sick fish. The best place to put a quarantine tank is in a quiet, secluded place in the house. The only equipment needed is only a heater and filter, as well as a clean container full of aquarium water (for sale in most aquarium shops). They tend to be smaller than the main tank.

Here is a chart for quarantine tank sizes (Note: G = gallons):

If you have a:	**10G**	use:	**5G**		If you have a:	**60G**	use:	**30G**
If you have a:	**20G**	use:	**5G**		If you have a:	**70G**	use:	**40G**
If you have a:	**30G**	use:	**10G**		If you have a:	**80G**	use:	**40G**
If you have a:	**40G**	use:	**10G**		If you have a:	**90G**	use:	**40G**
If you have a:	**50G**	use:	**20G**		If you have a:	**100G**	use:	**50G**

If you have a:	**Neon Tetra**	use: **5G**	If you have a:	**Common Pleco**	use: **55G**
If you have a:	**Corydoras**	use: **10G**	If you have a:	**Platy**	use: **5G**
If you have a:	**Dwarf Corydoras**	use: **5G**	If you have a:	**Betta**	use: **1G**
If you have a:	**Angelfish**	use: **20G**	If you have a:	**Molly**	use: **5G**
If you have a:	**Goldfish**	use: **20G**	If you have a:	**Swordtail**	use: **5G**
If you have a:	**Barb**	use: **30G**	If you have a:	**Guppy**	use: **1G**

Chapter 19: Medicine

One of the worst things you can do is buy medicine before fish get sick. This is like going to the pharmacy and buying every bottle on the shelf. When buying medicine, you should describe the disease to an experienced worker in a fish shop and buy what they recommend. I myself like KanaPlex™, useful for treating most any bacterial and fungal infections. Using practically any medicine is as simple as following the instructions on the package.

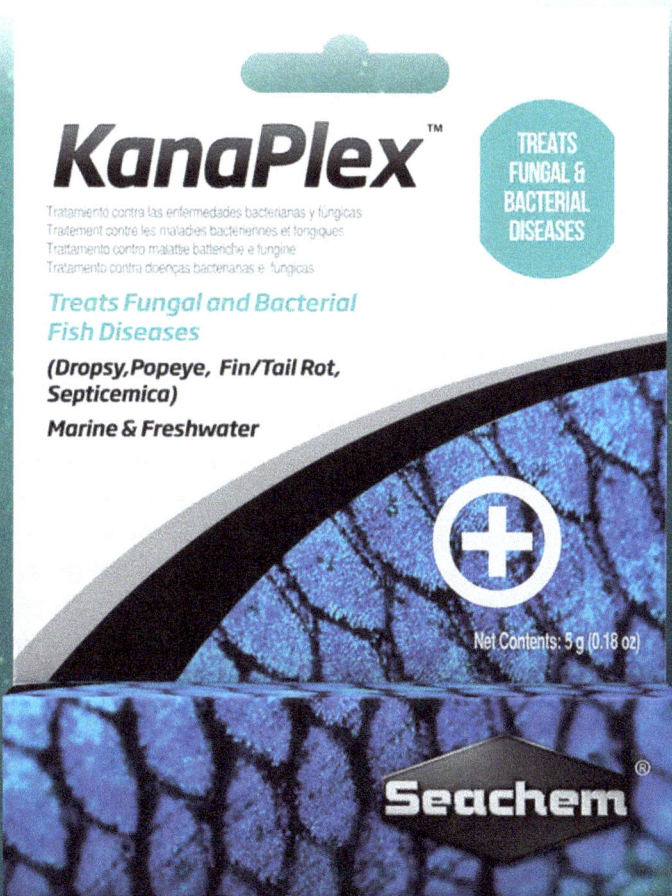

Chapter 20: When a Fish Dies

When a fish dies, you should remove it from the tank immediately. If left in a tank too long, it will decompose, and your ammonia levels will skyrocket. Dead fish can be buried as compost or simply flushed down the toilet.

Before disposing of a fish, take a moment to answer these questions:

- Does it have any visible body wounds? If it does, it may have been fighting with other fish.

- Does it have any signs of the diseases mentioned earlier? If so, go back and find out which one and go to your fish store for medicine. The diseases can spread from dead fish to live ones.

- Is it discolored? If so, it is possible it has been dead for a while.

- When you found it, was it trapped somewhere (in the filter, under a shell or rock, etc)? If it was, it may have starved and not have been able to escape.

- Is it whole? If not, and you only find a few pieces, it was most likely eaten. Check the Compatibility Chart in chapter 32.

If replacing schooling fish like tetras or barbs, you should put the fish that are in the main tank, as well as the new fish, into a quarantine tank and turn off the lights for the rest of the day. This reduces stress from aggression when adding fish. The next morning, return the lighting to normal. In a week or so, move all the fish in the main display tank. Again, turn off the lights for the rest of the day, and the next morning return to normal. This process should also be repeated when adding anything to the tank. This way, if you accidentally buy a sick fish you will not infect the entire main display. While not absolutely necessary with freshwater, this process MUST be followed with saltwater, because saltwater fish are so delicate.

DEAD FISH

Part 5: Model Setups*

Not all of these are model setups for beginners:. "B" means this is a setup suitable for beginners, "I" is for intermediate and "A" is advanced.

Chapter 21: Hardware and Software

"Hardware" in an aquarium refers to inorganic hard aquascaping materials, such as rocks and driftwood. For example, in a 55-gallon all-male peacock cichlid display, you might have driftwood, rocks and a stonier substrate. All of these are hardware. Hardware is mostly the foundation of an aquarium. For example, in a reef tank, most of the corals will be growing on live rock. The foundation is built, and then a layer of corals is grown on top. Software refers to organic matter, such as corals, macroalgae and plants. **Software** is often used to achieve color and diversity, especially in marine reef tanks.

HARDWARE   SOFTWARE

Fish Facts

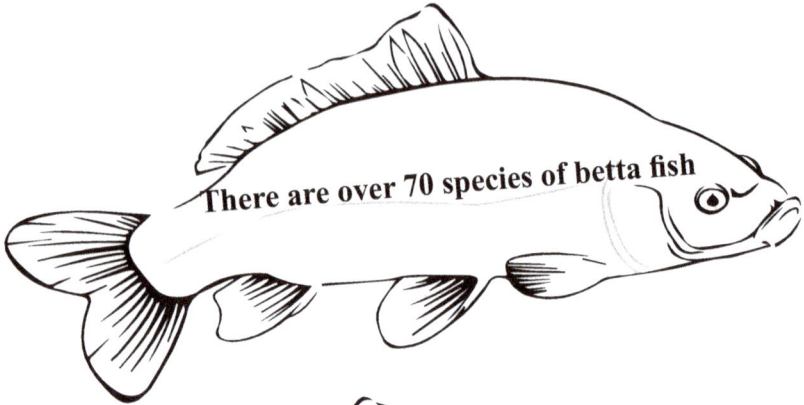

There are over 70 species of betta fish

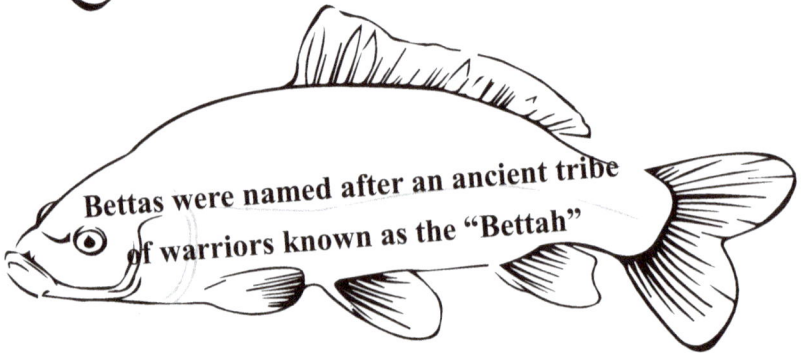

Bettas were named after an ancient tribe of warriors known as the "Bettah"

Bettas can breathe air, like humans

Chapter 22: Tropical 5 Gallon (B)

This low-maintenance tank features a betta as its main inhabitant. Use fine-grained sand, along with some easy-to-care-for plants, such as Java moss and moss balls. Use a small aerator along with a heater and good light. Do 30% water changes every week and feed the betta every day, preferably alternating between high quality flake foods and meatier foods, like brine shrimp. Provide the plants with necessary fertilizer.

Fish Facts

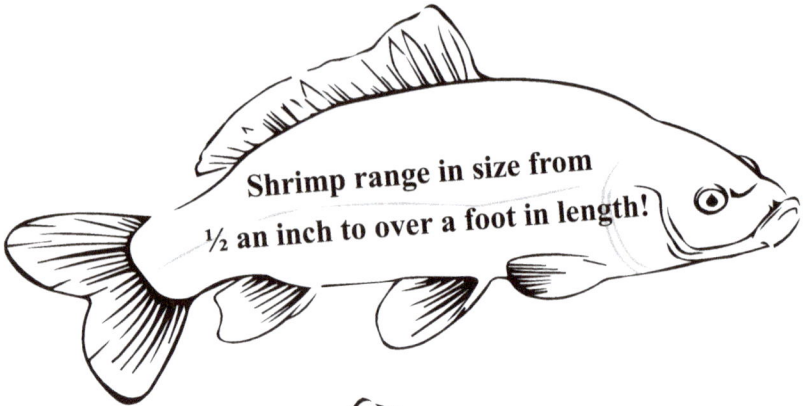

Shrimp range in size from ½ an inch to over a foot in length!

Shrimp are excellent swimmers

Some shrimp can make an extremely loud snapping noise

Chapter 23: 5 Gallon Asian Stream (B)

There are a lot of different shrimp out there, all beautiful. When I say shrimp, I am referring to dwarf shrimp, particularly neocaridina. The general stocking rule for dwarf shrimp is 10-12 shrimp per gallon, although five to six are best. Do 30% water changes every week. Provide shrimp with live plants, particularly "real" moss balls, compared to Java moss balls. Feed every day with algae tabs, treating them every week with high quality flake food or frozen shrimp preparations (the ones made for shrimp, not from shrimp).

Fish Facts

Pea puffer fish don't have scales

Oto catfish eat algae

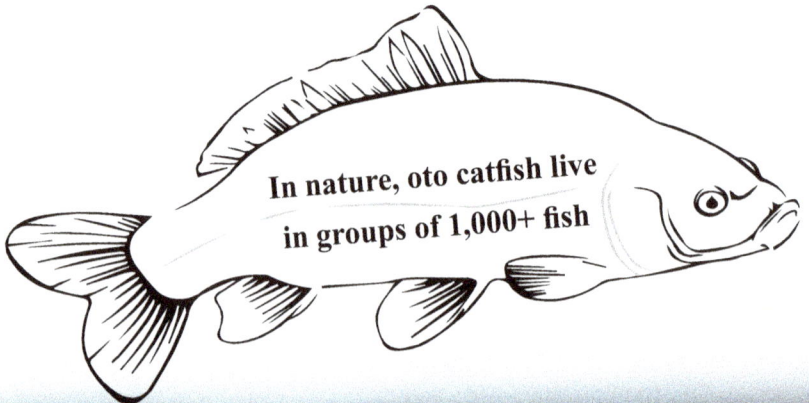

In nature, oto catfish live in groups of 1,000+ fish

Chapter 24: Planted Pea Puffer 10 Gallon (B)

This tank features a trio of pea pufferfish as centerpiece fish, as well as a trio of otocinclus (oto) catfish. Some aquarists find otos hard to care for, but otos were my very first fish, along with ember tetras. The otos will eat algae tabs and other foods for herbivores, while the pufferfish should be fed brine shrimp or krill every day. Pea puffers MUST have a densely planted tank. Do 30% water changes every week.

OTO CATFISH

PEA PUFFERFISH

Fish Facts

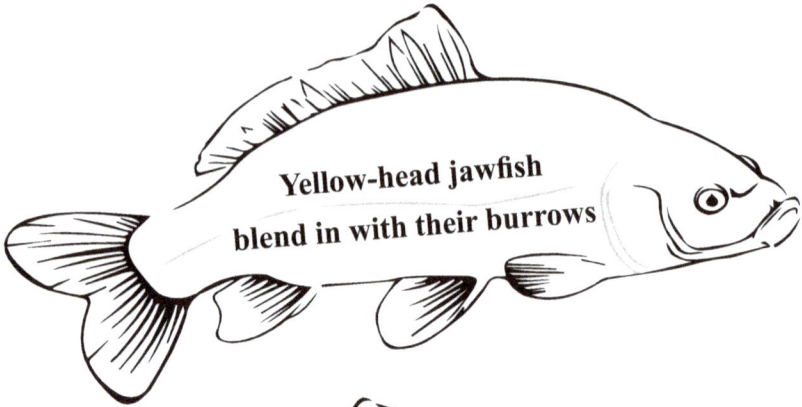

Yellow-head jawfish blend in with their burrows

Shrimp gobies live in mud burrows

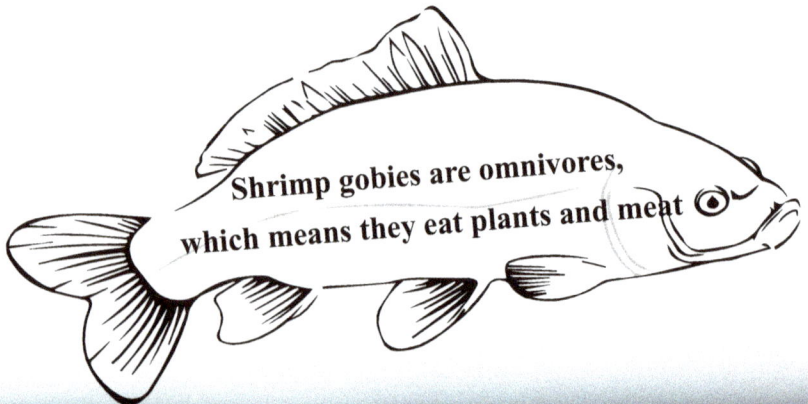

Shrimp gobies are omnivores, which means they eat plants and meat

Chapter 25: 20 Gallon Ocean Floor (I)

This community features a yellowhead jawfish and the ever-popular shrimp goby, in this case the yasha shrimp goby. The jawfish needs at least four inches of sand to dig its burrow, and some live rock to use as the roof of the burrow. Feed at least once daily, alternating between high quality flake food meant specifically for marine fish and frozen mysis or brine shrimp. Corals are optional, good choices are button polyps or zoanthids. Do 30% water changes every week, and mix saltwater with commercial mix at least one day ahead of time.

Fish Facts

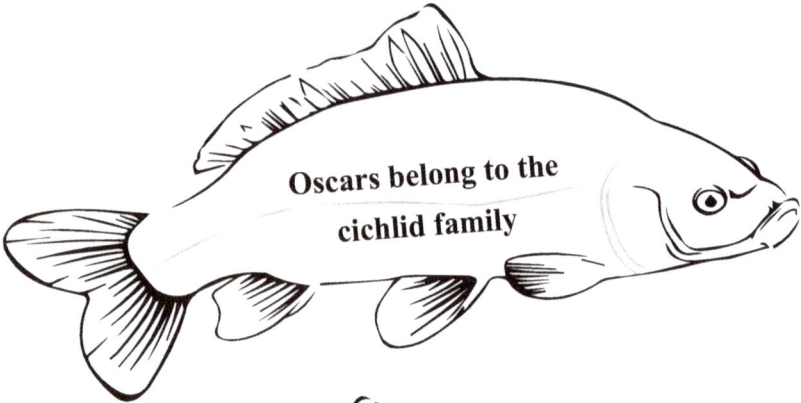

Oscars belong to the cichlid family

Oscars are one of the smartest fish

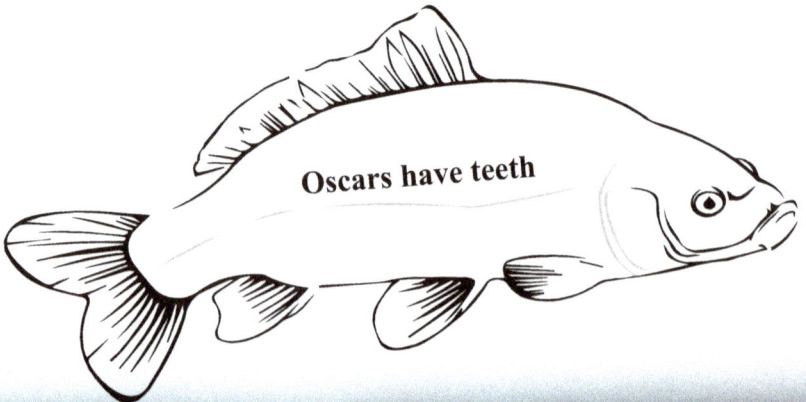

Oscars have teeth

Chapter 26: 75 Gallon Oscar Tank (I)

Oscars are a large fish, growing over one foot long, and are mischievous. They have been reported to dig up plants and throw rocks around, and in general are destructive fish. Keep them in solitary in a 75-gallon tank. Oscars are just as much of an intelligent pet as cats or dogs. They are very aware of their surroundings, and will even learn to eat from your hands! Alternate feeding them cichlid pellets and live feeder fish. Feed your oscar every day and do a 30% water change every week.

Fish Facts

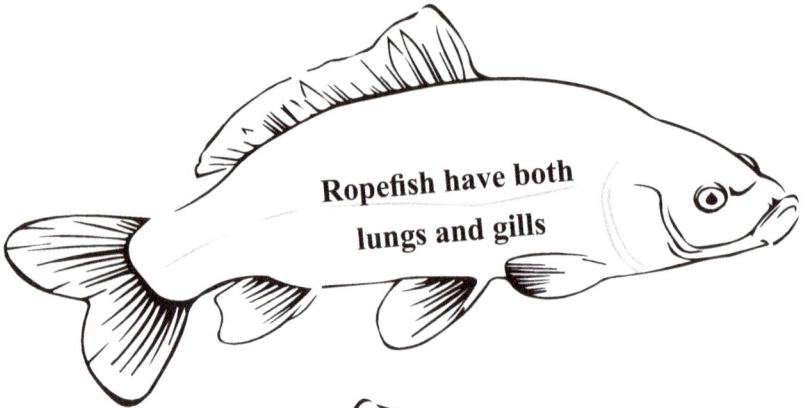

Ropefish have both lungs and gills

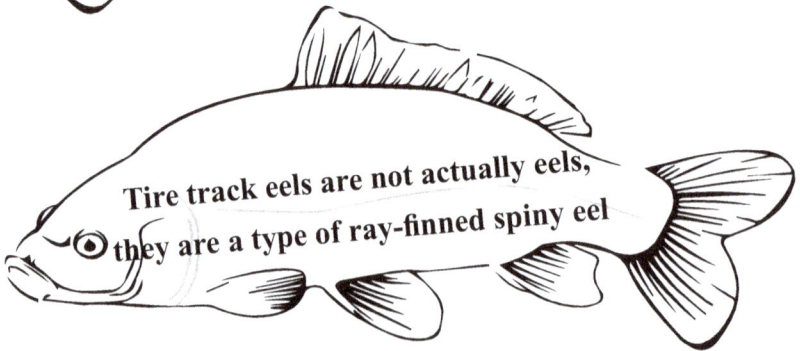

Tire track eels are not actually eels, they are a type of ray-finned spiny eel

Red devil cichlids grow up to 15 inches

Chapter 27: 75 Gallon Display Tank (I)

This tank is an oddball tank, full of unique fish with personality. It features 3 ropefish, a red devil cichlid and a tire track eel. All of these fish will need to be fed meaty foods, and will appreciate live foods. Feed your fish every other day and do a 30% water change every week.

ROPEFISH

TIRE TRACK EEL

RED DEVIL
CICHLID

Fish Facts

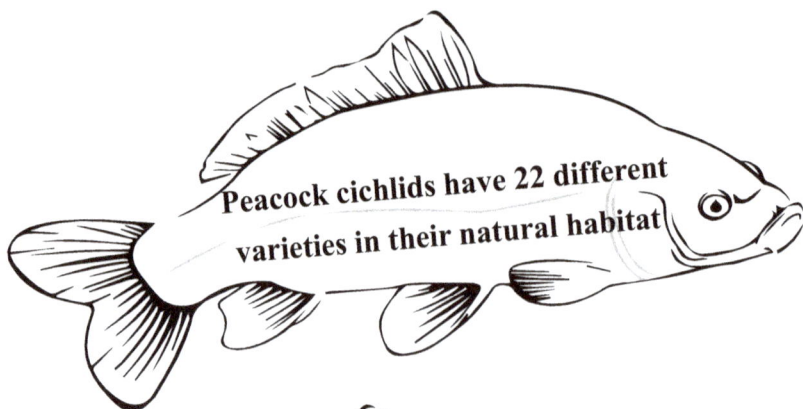

Peacock cichlids have 22 different varieties in their natural habitat

There are 28 species of peacock cichlid

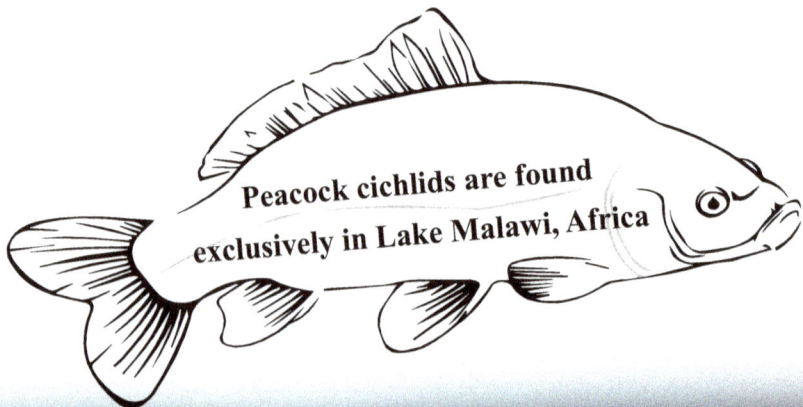

Peacock cichlids are found exclusively in Lake Malawi, Africa

Chapter 28: 80 Gallon Cichlid Tank (I)

Take special care to only get males for this all-male peacock cichlid display tank. This tank features three blue, three yellow, three red and three albino peacock cichlids. Alternate feeding them bloodworms, live feeder fish and high quality cichlid pellets. Pay attention while feeding them: if one is bullied to the point that it won't eat, you will have to feed it in your quarantine tank. Use only rocks, driftwood and sand in this tank--and no software (plants). Do a 30% water change every week.

PEACOCK CICHLID

Fish Facts

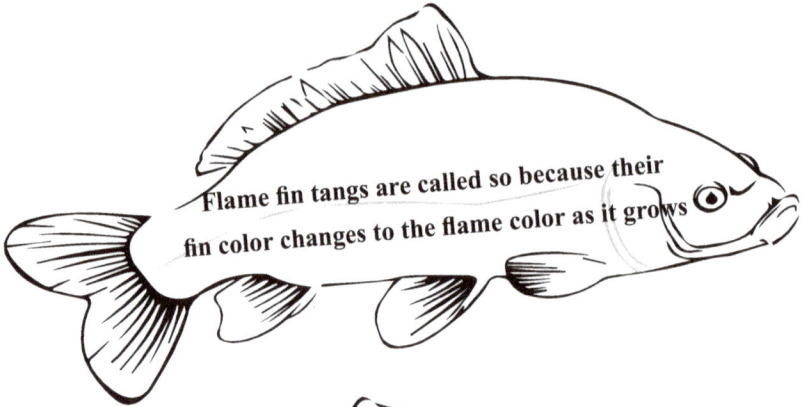

Flame fin tangs are called so because their fin color changes to the flame color as it grows

Snowflake eels are escape artists

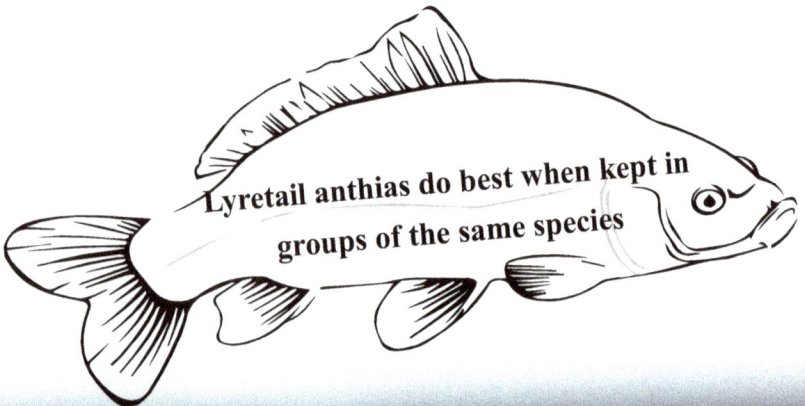

Lyretail anthias do best when kept in groups of the same species

FLAME FIN
TOMINI TANG

LYRETAIL ANTHIAS

Chapter 29: 80 Gallon Reef (A)

This tank features a trio of lyretail anthias (two females and a male), a flame fin tomini tang and a snowflake eel. The tang will need to be fed nori (dried seaweed), lettuce and preparations for herbivores, while the eel will need to be fed krill or silversides with feeding tongs. Alternate feeding your anthias frozen mysis or brine shrimp and high-quality flake food meant specifically for marine fish. Do a 30% water change every week.

SNOWFLAKE
EEL

Part 6: Maintenance

Chapter 30: Feeding

There is no magic formula for how much to feed your fish, this must be decided by trial and error.

I have seen many recommendations on how much to feed fish, including these:

- feed them twice daily with no more than they can consume in two minutes,

- feed them once daily with no more than they can consume in two minutes or

- feed them every other day with no more than they can consume in five minutes.

These "rules" should be considered guidelines. I find feeding a small pinch of food per day per non-bottom dwelling fish works best (a pinch and a half if you have scavengers, in my case corydoras catfish). For example, in my 10-gallon tank, with a zebra danio, four bloodfin tetras and three bronze corydoras catfish, I feed two solid pinches of bloodworms or flakes, alternating between the two, directly into the filter flow. I do have a white freshwater lobster, which is really just a crawfish, and I feed her twice a day alternating between algae wafers and frozen krill. Of course, if she is gnawing on my fake plants, I feed algae wafers. If she is eyeballing my fish, I feed her krill. She will "beg" for food, as she is doing now as I type this very sentence, climbing up the glass (or at least trying to).

There are many types of foods available for the beginning aquarist. In fact, so many that choosing can seem daunting.

FISH EATING

Chapter 31: Flake Food

One common type of food is flake food. Available in many types, you must be sure to get a high quality flake food, as there are some very sketchy products out there. When feeding marine fish flake food, make sure it is meant specifically for marine fish, with marine ingredients. Some flake food has natural color-enhancing pigments in it, and these are to be sought out. They help enhance and develop the colors of your fish. There are also spirulina (a type of algae) flake food for herbivores, as well as nori (dried seaweed) and algae tabs.

PILE OF FLAKE FOOD

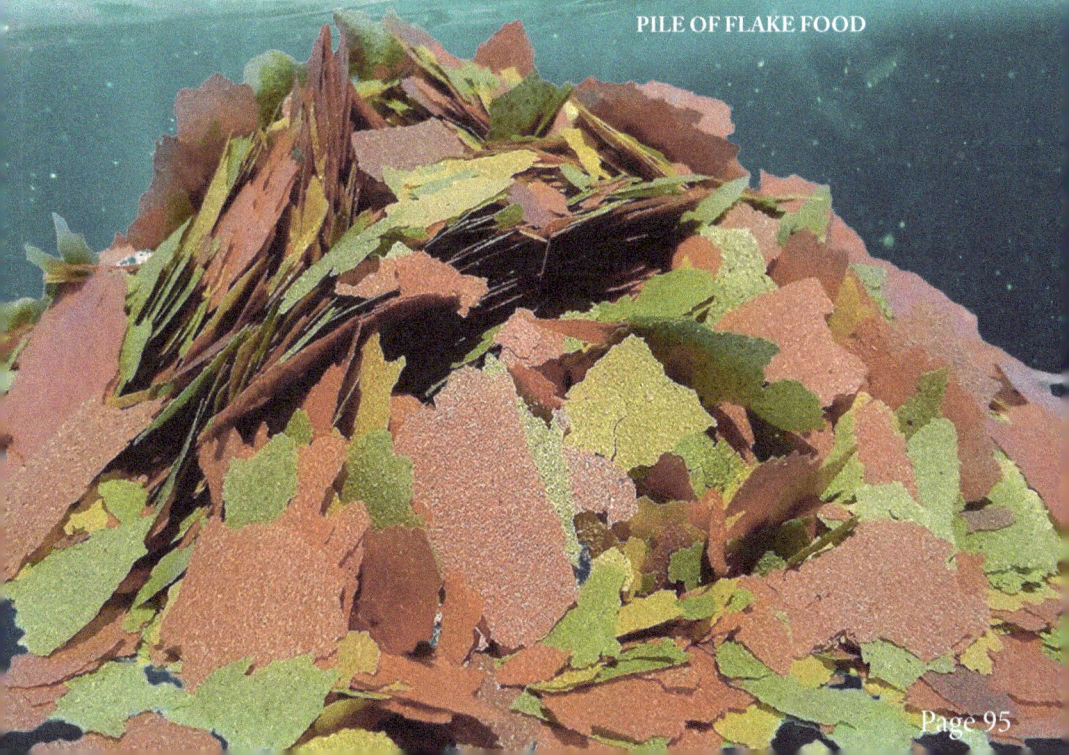

Chapter 32: Live Food

All non-herbivorous fish will eat live foods. Live foods are most often used to train picky fish to eat frozen, or in worst-case scenarios used to feed fish permanently. Baby brine shrimp is one of the best live foods for fish. Dried brine shrimp eggs can be bought very inexpensively, and can easily be hatched by being submerged in a tank meant for raising them, WITH NO FISH. You can also raise feeder guppies. You can try to raise feeder goldfish, but they aren't the best option. They are generally unhealthy and sometimes even sick.

BABY BRINE SHRIMP

Chapter 33: Frozen Food

Bloodworms are insect larvae. I prefer the freeze-dried variety (and some frozen) because they are "safe," meaning that they are parasite-free. Mysis shrimp can be a good choice for pickier saltwater fish. Silversides are good for carnivores, so long as there are no similarly sized fish. If there are, your carnivore won't be able to tell the difference between said fish and its food. As you can imagine, that wouldn't go well.

FROZEN BLOODWORM CUBES

When it comes to pickier fish and carnivorous fish, it works best to train fish. To train fish, feed a ratio of 9:1 of live foods to frozen foods. Increase the amount of frozen foods by one while decreasing the amount of live foods by one every other day to every week. If the fish doesn't eat the new formula, go back to the previous formula for a couple of days before trying again. If all goes well, your fish will be eating frozen foods in a few months.

Chapter 34: Water Changes

When it comes to water changes, you should do them every week. The percent changed ranges from 5% to 50% to even 100%. I try to avoid changing too much for two reasons. One, the obvious reason, is that it is a waste of time and energy, and the more you take out, the more stressful it is to the fish. The second reason is because of something called the "yoyo effect." Remember that beneficial bacteria way back at the beginning of the book? Well, if you are siphoning like you are supposed to, and do too big of a water change, you remove too much of the beneficial bacteria, and then your tank, at least temporarily, becomes overstocked. Every six months, I do a 75% water change. You should also treat your tap water with a dechlorinator. You want the dechlorinator you use to actually say it removes chloramine. If it removes chloramine then it removes chlorine, but not vice versa.

A siphon is a useful tool for doing water changes in the aquarium. It is a long tube with a larger tube on the end. You bob it up and down in the water, pounding it into the gravel but not letting the gravel get out of the tube. In doing this, you create a vacuum that sucks the water through the tube into a container, where it can be disposed of. You should not use a siphon in a heavily planted tank, as it will damage the root system of the plants. I use a five-gallon bucket and a siphon to do my water changes.

Chapter 35: Filter Maintenance

Some filters have a sponge that doesn't require replacements, but most commonly available filters have activated carbon. Activated carbon, but NOT the filter cartridges, needs to be replaced every month. Sometimes, in a heavily enough stocked tank, the filter cartridge gets full of gunk. Instead of replacing it, I wash it off with a faucet on spray mode.

Cleaning the filter is something you should do every month. I unplug the filter, lay it down on a towel, disassemble the filter and wipe it down with a wet paper towel. I also use a faucet on spray on the inside of the filter. Sometimes, you may have to replace your filter. Hopefully you won't have to do this, but I already have once and plan to again. My first replacement took place when I first started out and had bought a cheap, low quality Walmart filter. I replaced it with a filter from my LFS (local fish store), Wet Pets.

Fishpedia Freshwater

Arowana, Platinum

Common name: Platinum Arowana

Scientific name: *Osteoglossidae*

Habitat: Breeding facilities

Size: 2-3'

Diet: Carnivore

Parameters: 7 pH

Compatibility: Large, aggressive fish

Tank size: 350 gallons

Temperament: Aggressive

Price range: $200,000-$300,000

Life span: 10-15 years

Buying tips: It's hard to find one of these.

Platinum Arowana

Fishpedia Freshwater

Bala Shark

Common name: Bala Shark

Scientific name: *Cyprinidae*

Habitat: Rivers and streams

Size: 12-14"

Diet: Omnivore

Parameters: 7 pH

Compatibility: Anything able to put up with a large, active, schooling fish

Tank size: 125 gallons

Temperament: Peaceful

Price range: $5-$25

Life span: 8-10 years

Buying tips: They should have no white spots, nor should any other fish in the tank.

Bala Shark

Fishpedia **Freshwater**

Barbs

Common name: Barbs

Scientific name: *Cyprinidae*

Habitat: Small creeks

Size: 1.5-12"

Diet: Omnivore

Parameters: 7 pH

Compatibility: Fish with short fins and semi-aggressive

Tank size: 10-100 gallons

Temperament: Semi-aggressive

Price range: $2-$20

Life span: 7 years

Buying tips: In general, if a barb isn't moving it's not healthy.

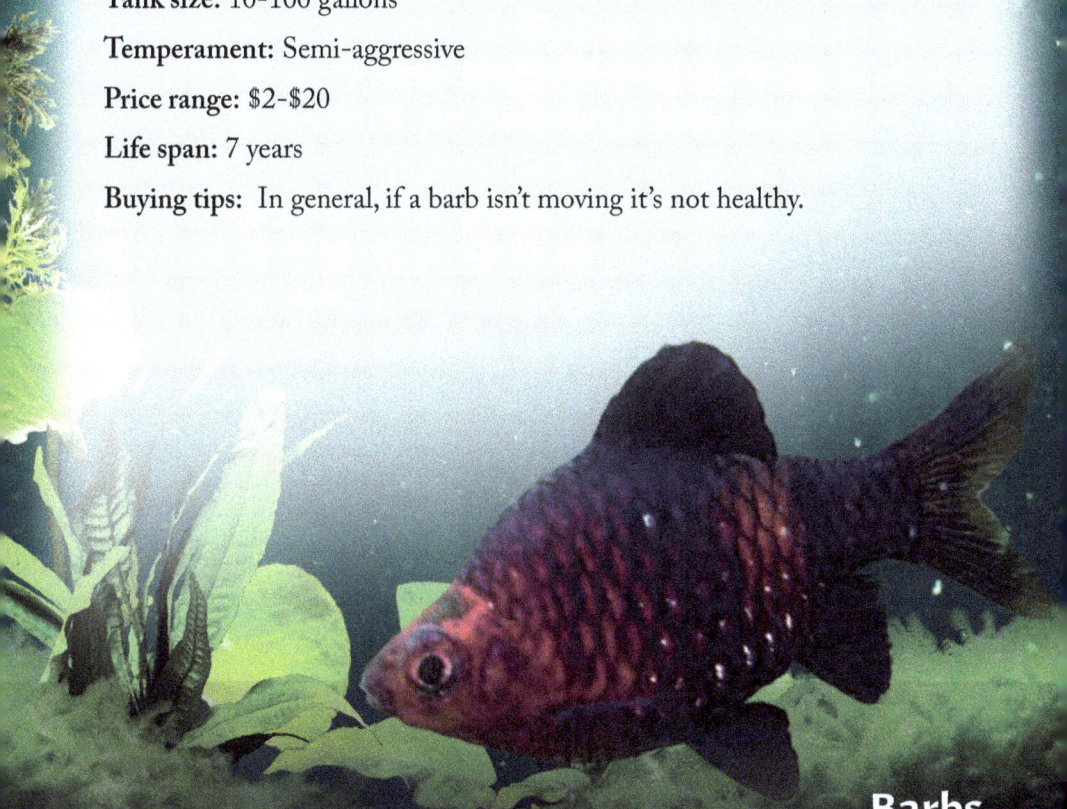

Barbs

Fishpedia Freshwater

Betta and Gourami

Common name: Betta, Gourami

Scientific name: *Osphronemidae*

Habitat: Slow-moving rivers, swamps, fields, and pools

Size: 2-5"

Diet: Omnivore

Parameters: 7 pH

Compatibility: Slow-moving, peaceful fish

Tank size: 20-55 gallons

Temperament: Peaceful, shy

Price range: $10-$20

Life span: 3-5 years

Buying tips: Make sure all their fins are intact.

Betta and Gourami

Fishpedia Freshwater

Cichlids

Common name: Cichlids

Scientific name: *Cichlidae*

Habitat: Large bodies of freshwater

Size: 6-18"

Diet: Omnivore

Parameters: 7 pH

Compatibility: Hard, large catfish, other similar-size cichlids

Tank size: 55-75 gallons

Temperament: Aggressive

Price range: $5-$50

Life span: 10 years

Buying tips: Make sure you choose fish with the correct body proportions for the species.

Cichlids

Fishpedia Freshwater

Corydoras

Common name: Corydoras

Scientific name: *Callichthyidae*

Habitat: South America, bottoms of small rivers/streams

Size: 1-5"

Diet: Omnivore

Parameters: 7 pH

Compatibility: Any non-aggressive fish

Tank size: 10-20 gallons

Temperament: Peaceful

Price range: $4-$50

Life span: 3-5 years

Buying tips: They should be foraging around for food.

Corydoras

Fishpedia Freshwater

Crab, Panther

Common name: Panther Crab

Scientific name: *Gecarcinucidae*

Habitat: Streams and rivers

Size: 2-3"

Diet: Omnivore

Parameters: 7 pH

Compatibility: In general, panther crabs can only live with panther crabs

Tank size: 10 gallons

Temperament: Aggressive

Price range: $20-$30

Life span: Up to 10 years

Buying tips: They should be crawling around the bottom with a complete shell.

Panther Crab

Fishpedia Freshwater

Crab, Thai Micro

Common name: Thai micro crab

Scientific name: *Hymenosomatidae*

Habitat: Streams and rivers

Size: 0.25-0.5"

Diet: Omnivore

Parameters: 7 pH

Compatibility: Anything too small to eat it.

Tank size: 5 gallons

Temperament: Peaceful

Price range: $5-$10

Life span: 1.5-2 years

Buying tips: They should be crawling around the bottom with a complete shell.

Thai Micro Crab

Fishpedia Freshwater

Crayfish

Common name: Crayfish

Scientific name: *Astacidae / Parastacidae / Austroastracidae*

Habitat: Rivers

Size: 1-8"

Diet: Omnivore

Parameters: 7 pH

Compatibility: Fish too fast for it to catch

Tank size: 10-55 gallons

Temperament: Aggressive

Price range: $5-$20

Life span: 1-20+ years

Buying tips: They should be hiding/crawling around with an intact shell.

Crayfish

Fishpedia Freshwater

Goldfish

Common name: Goldfish

Scientific name: *Cyprinidae*

Habitat: Rivers and ponds

Size: 6-12"

Diet: Omnivore

Parameters: 7 pH

Compatibility: Medium-sized, coldwater fish

Tank size: 20-55 gallons

Temperament: Peaceful

Price range: $0.20-$50

Life span: 10-15 years

Buying tips: Don't buy 20¢ feeder goldfish- they will most likely die.

Goldfish

Fishpedia Freshwater

Killifish

Common name: Killifish

Scientific name: *Fundulus*

Habitat: Ponds and puddles

Size: 1-6"

Diet: Omnivore

Parameters: 7 pH

Compatibility: Best kept alone

Tank size: 5-30 gallons

Temperament: Peaceful

Price range: $5-$50

Life span: 1-5 years

Buying tips: They should be small and young- around half of all killifish only live for one year.

Killifish

Fishpedia Freshwater

Knifefish

Common name: Knifefish

Scientific name: *Apteronotidae*

Habitat: Rivers

Size: 12-36"

Diet: Omnivore

Parameters: 7 pH

Compatibility: Fish too big for it to eat

Tank size: 55-120 gallons

Temperament: Peaceful, shy

Price range: $10-$40

Life span: 10-15 years

Buying tips: The tank should have some plastic tubes for the knifefish to hide in.

Knifefish

Fishpedia **Freshwater**

Livebearers

Common name: Livebearers

Scientific name: *Poeciliidae*

Habitat: Small, slow-moving creeks and streams

Size: 1-5"

Diet: Omnivore

Parameters: 7 pH

Compatibility: Medium-size, calm, peaceful fish

Tank size: 10-30 gallons

Temperament: Peaceful

Price range: free-$30

Life span: 3-5 years

Buying tips: Keep an eye out for ripped fins.

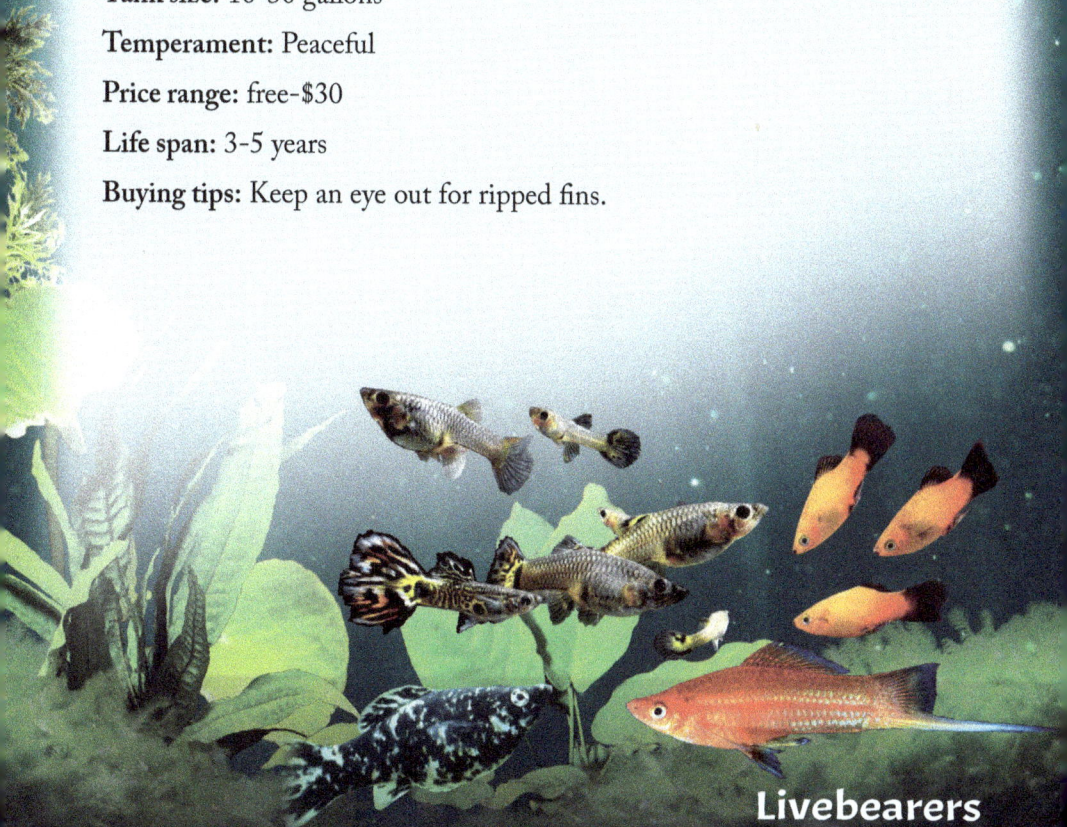

Livebearers

Fishpedia Freshwater

Loaches

Common name: Loaches

Scientific name: *Cobitidae*

Habitat: Streams and rivers

Size: 1-12"

Diet: Omnivore

Parameters: 7 pH

Compatibility: Peaceful, robust fish

Tank size: 10-120 gallons

Temperament: Peaceful

Price range: $5-$50

Life span: 7-10 years

Buying tips: Make sure they have no white spots

Loaches

Fishpedia **Freshwater**

Pleco

Common name: Pleco

Scientific name: *Loricariidae*

Habitat: Streams and rivers

Size: 3-18"

Diet: Herbivore

Parameters: 7 pH

Compatibility: Small-medium sized fish; some medium and most large fish will become targets to the pleco, and have their slime coats sucked off (this will kill them)

Tank size: 10-200 gallons

Temperament: Peaceful (see compatibility)

Price range: $5-$200

Life span: 10-15 years

Buying tips: They should be cleaning the aquarium.

Fishpedia Freshwater

Shrimp

Common name: Shrimp

Scientific name: *Caridea*

Habitat: Rivers and streams

Size: 1"

Diet: Omnivore

Parameters: 7 pH

Compatibility: Fish that are too small to eat them or who won't eat them

Tank size: 5 gallons

Temperament: Peaceful

Price range: $1-$20

Life span: 2-6 years

Buying tips: They should be foraging around the walls, plants, and decorations.

Shrimp

Fishpedia Freshwater

Shrimp, Amano

Common name: Amano shrimp

Scientific name: *Atyidae*

Habitat: Rivers and creeks

Size: 2"

Diet: Herbivore

Parameters: 7 pH

Compatibility: Fish too small to eat it.

Tank size: 10 gallons

Temperament: Peaceful

Price range: $5-$20

Life span: 2-3 years

Buying tips: They should be foraging for algae on decorations.

Amano Shrimp

Fishpedia Freshwater

Snail, Apple

Common name: Apple Snail

Scientific name: *Ampullariidae*

Habitat: Ponds and rivers

Size: 6"

Diet: Omnivore

Parameters: 7 pH

Compatibility: Anything that doesn't eat snails

Tank size: 30 gallons

Temperament: Peaceful

Price range: $5-$15

Life span: 1-3 years, the colder the water the longer they live

Buying tips: They should have an intact shell.

Apple Snail

Fishpedia **Freshwater**

Snail, Mystery

Common name: Mystery Snail

Scientific name: *Ampullariidae*

Habitat: Rivers and streams

Size: 1-2"

Diet: Omnivore, true scavengers

Parameters: 7 pH

Compatibility: Anything that doesn't eat snails

Tank size: 10 gallons

Temperament: Peaceful

Price range: $2-$10

Life span: 1 year

Buying tips: They should have a complete, intact shell, fully colored.

Mystery Snail

Fishpedia Freshwater

Tetras

Common name: Tetras

Scientific name: *Characidae*

Habitat: Small, slow-moving creeks and streams

Size: 1-3"

Diet: Omnivore

Parameters: 7 pH

Compatibility: Peaceful, non-predatory fish

Tank size: 10-30 gallons

Temperament: Peaceful

Price range: $2-$20

Life span: 5 years

Buying tips: If there are sick fish in the tank, ones with a much paler color or dead fish, move on.

Tetras

Fishpedia Saltwater

Anemone, Sea

Common name: Sea Anemone

Scientific name: *Cnidaria* (there are 46 different families)

Habitat: Reefs

Size: 2-24"

Diet: Carnivore

Parameters: 8 pH

Compatibility: Anything too big for it to eat

Tank size: 10-30 gallons

Temperament: Peaceful

Price range: $10-$30

Life span: 3-5 years

Buying tips: It should have its tentacles fully extended.

Sea Anemone

Fishpedia Saltwater

Angelfish, Dwarf

Common name: Dwarf Angelfish

Scientific name: *Pomacanthidae*

Habitat: Reefs

Size: 4-5"

Diet: Omnivore

Parameters: 8 pH

Compatibility: Semi-aggressive, medium-sized fish

Tank size: 55 gallons

Temperament: Semi-aggressive

Price range: $20-$120

Life span: up to 15 years

Buying tips: They should glide in and out of rockwork.

Dwarf Angelfish

Fishpedia **Saltwater**

Angelfish, Peppermint

Common name: Peppermint Angelfish

Scientific name: *Pomacanthidae*

Habitat: Reefs

Size: 4-5"

Diet: Omnivore

Parameters: 8 pH

Compatibility: Medium-sized, semi-aggressive fish

Tank size: 55 gallons

Temperament: Semi-aggressive

Price range: $20,000-$30,000

Life span: 10-15 years

Buying tips: It's hard to find one of these.

Peppermint Angelfish

Fishpedia Saltwater

Anthias

Common name: Anthias

Scientific name: *Serranidae*

Habitat: Reefs

Size: 4-6"

Diet: Omnivore

Parameters: 7 pH

Compatibility: Peaceful, slow-eating fish

Tank size: 55 gallons

Temperament: Peaceful

Price range: $20-$50

Life span: 5-6 years

Buying tips: They should be colorful and active.

Anthias

Fishpedia Saltwater

Betta, Marine

Common name: Marine betta

Scientific name: *Plesiopidae*

Habitat: Reefs

Size: 6-8"

Diet: Carnivore

Parameters: 8 pH

Compatibility: Anything too big for it to eat, 2"+

Tank size: 55 gallons

Temperament: Peaceful

Price range: $20-$50

Life span: 10+ years

Buying tips: They won't be very active in the store.

Marine Betta

Fishpedia **Saltwater**

Butterflyfish

Common name: Butterflyfish

Scientific name: *Chaetodontidae*

Habitat: Reefs

Size: 6-12"

Diet: Omnivore

Parameters: 8 pH

Compatibility: Anything that won't nip its fins

Tank size: 55-120 gallons

Temperament: Peaceful

Price range: $25-$125

Life span: 5-7 years

Buying tips: Ask someone to feed the fish, only buy it if it eats.

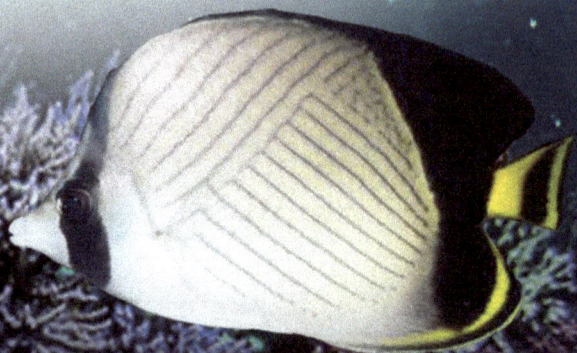

Butterflyfish

Fishpedia Saltwater

Clownfish (Damselfish, Chromis)

Common name: Clownfish, Damselfish, Chromis

Scientific name: *Pomacentridae*

Habitat: Reefs

Size: 1-6"

Diet: Omnivore

Parameters: 8 pH

Compatibility: Semi-aggressive fish

Tank size: 10-55 gallons

Temperament: Semi-aggressive to aggressive

Price range: $10-$100

Life span: 4-6 years

Buying tips: They should be vibrant and colorful.

Clownfish/Damselfish/Chromis

Fishpedia Saltwater

Crab, Arrow

Common name: Arrow Crab

Scientific name: *Inachidae*

Habitat: Reefs

Size: 4-12"

Diet: Omnivore

Parameters: 8 pH

Compatibility: Anything too big for it to eat

Tank size: 10 gallons

Temperament: Semi-aggressive

Price range: $10-$25

Life span: 3-5 years

Buying tips: They should have all their limbs..

Arrow Crab

Fishpedia **Saltwater**

Crab, Emerald

Common name: Emerald Crab

Scientific name: *Majidae*

Habitat: Reefs

Size: 1-2"

Diet: Omnivore

Parameters: 8 pH

Compatibility: Anything too small to eat them

Tank size: 10 gallons

Temperament: Semi-aggressive

Price range: $5-$20

Life span: 2-4 years

Buying tips: They come in many shades that don't look normal but are, such as ones that are almost white and others that are red/purple.

Emerald Crab

Fishpedia Saltwater

Crab, Hermit

Common name: Hermit Crab

Scientific name: *Coenobitidae*

Habitat: Reefs

Size: 1-3"

Diet: Omnivore

Parameters: 8 pH

Compatibility: Fish that don't eat crabs

Tank size: 10 gallons

Temperament: Peaceful

Price range: $5-$30

Life span: 2-5 years

Buying tips: They should be wearing a shell.

Hermit Crab

Fishpedia **Saltwater**

Eels

Common name: Eels

Scientific name: *Muraenidae*

Habitat: Reefs

Size: 12-24"

Diet: Carnivore

Parameters: 8 pH

Compatibility: Anything too big for it to eat

Tank size: 55 gallons

Temperament: Peaceful

Price range: $20-$60

Life span: 15+ years

Buying tips: It should be coiled around/in a rock.

Eels

Fishpedia Saltwater

Firefish

Common name: Firefish

Scientific name: *Gobiidae*

Habitat: Reefs

Size: 3-4"

Diet: Omnivore

Parameters: 8 pH

Compatibility: Small, shy fish

Tank size: 10 gallons

Temperament: Peaceful

Price range: $15-$30

Life span: 3-5 years

Buying tips: They should be constantly flexing their fins and darting in and out of rockwork.

Firefish

Fishpedia Saltwater

Goby

Common name: Goby

Scientific name: *Gobiidae*

Habitat: Bottoms of reefs

Size: 1-5"

Diet: Omnivore

Parameters: 8 pH

Compatibility: Peaceful fish

Tank size: 10-40 gallons

Temperament: Peaceful

Price range: $10-$50

Life span: 1-10 years

Buying tips: They should be perched on/fluttering around rocks.

Goby

Fishpedia Saltwater

Grouper

Common name: Grouper

Scientific name: *Serranidae*

Habitat: Reefs

Size: 1-8'

Diet: Carnivore

Parameters: 8 pH

Compatibility: Anything too big for it to eat

Tank size: 120-1,000 gallons

Temperament: Peaceful, can hold their own against aggressive fish

Price range: $40-$240

Life span: 20-25 years

Buying tips: They won't be very active.

Grouper

Fishpedia **Saltwater**

Jawfish

Common name: Jawfish

Scientific name: *Opistognathidae*

Habitat: Reefs

Size: 2-4"

Diet: Omnivore

Parameters: 8 pH

Compatibility: Peaceful fish

Tank size: 10-20 gallons

Temperament: Peaceful

Price range: $20-$50

Life span: 3-5 years

Buying tips: If they haven't dug a tunnel in the display tank, it's not a problem.

Jawfish

Fishpedia Saltwater

Lionfish

Common name: Lionfish

Scientific name: *Scorpaenidae*

Habitat: Reef

Size: 4-12"

Diet: Carnivore

Parameters: 8 pH

Compatibility: Everything except larger, aggressive fish and fish 2" and under

Tank size: 55-120 gallons

Temperament: Peaceful

Price range: $20-$50

Life span: 5-8 years

Buying tips: They should be slower-moving than other fish.

Lionfish

Fishpedia Saltwater

Pipefish

Common name: Pipefish

Scientific name: *Syngnathidae*

Habitat: Reefs

Size: 3-7"

Diet: Carnivore

Parameters: 8 pH

Compatibility: Small, shy fish that won't out-compete it for food

Tank size: 30-55 gallons

Temperament: Peaceful, shy

Price range: $20-$120

Life span: 5-10 years

Buying tips: They should be picking at the sand and rocks.

Fishpedia Saltwater

Lobster, Reef

Common name: Reef Lobster

Scientific name: *Enoplometopus*

Habitat: Reefs

Size: 4-5"

Diet: Omnivore

Parameters: 8 pH

Compatibility: Fish too big for it to eat

Tank size: 55 gallons

Temperament: Semi-aggressive

Price range: $20-$50

Life span: 10-12 years

Buying tips: They should be alert and bright.

Reef Lobster

Fishpedia Saltwater

Mandarin Fish

Common name: Mandarin Fish, Blue Mandarin

Scientific name: *Callionymidae*

Habitat: Reefs

Size: 3-4"

Diet: Carnivore- they only eat copepods

Parameters: 8 pH

Compatibility: Fish that don't eat copepods, fish that do will out-compete them for food.

Tank size: 55 gallons

Temperament: Peaceful

Price range: $10-$40

Life span: 10-15 years

Buying tips: They should be fluttering around, picking at the sand and rocks.

Mandarin Fish

Fishpedia Saltwater

Octopus

Common name: Octopus

Scientific name: *Octopodidae*

Habitat: Reefs

Size: 6-8"

Diet: Carnivore

Parameters: 8 pH

Compatibility: Best kept alone

Tank size: 30 gallons

Temperament: Aggressive

Price range: $25-$80

Life span: 6-12 months

Buying tips: Make sure the one you buy is double sealed in a bag, so it can't get out.

Octopus

Fishpedia **Saltwater**

Pufferfish

Common name: Pufferfish

Scientific name: *Tetraodontidae*

Habitat: Reefs

Size: 4-24"

Diet: Carnivore, needs hard things like clams to eat to keep their teeth trimmed.

Parameters: 8 pH

Compatibility: Medium-sized, semi-aggressive fish

Tank size: 30-550 gallons

Temperament: Semi-aggressive

Price range: $20-$50

Life span: 6-10 years

Buying tips: They shouldn't be inflated.

Pufferfish

Fishpedia Saltwater

Sea Cucumber

Common name: Sea Cucumber

Scientific name: *Holothuriidae*

Habitat: Reefs

Size: 3-12"

Diet: Omnivore

Parameters: 8 pH

Compatibility: Anything that doesn't make them feel threatened

Tank size: 30-100 gallons

Temperament: Peaceful

Price range: $20-$80

Life span: 5-10 years

Buying tips: Make sure the one you buy has a round sausage shape.

Sea Cucumber

Fishpedia **Saltwater**

Sea Slug

Common name: Sea Slug

Scientific name: *Opisthobranchs*

Habitat: Reefs

Size: 2-6"

Diet: Herbivore

Parameters: 8 pH

Compatibility: Anything that won't eat them

Tank size: 10-30 gallons

Temperament: Peaceful

Price range: $10-$30

Life span: 1 year

Buying tips: They should be slowly moving around.

Sea Slug

Fishpedia Saltwater

Seahorses

Common name: Seahorses

Scientific name: *Syngnathidae*

Habitat: Reefs

Size: 2-10"

Diet: Carnivore

Parameters: 8 pH

Compatibility: Small, shy fish that won't out-compete it for food

Tank size: 10-55 gallons

Temperament: Peaceful, shy

Price range: $25-$125

Life span: 1-5 years

Buying tips: They should be picking at the sand and rocks or perching on a rock/coral.

Seahorses

Fishpedia Saltwater

Shrimp, Camel

Common name: Camel Shrimp

Scientific name: *Rhynchocinetidae*

Habitat: Reefs

Size: 2-3"

Diet: Carnivore

Parameters: 8 pH

Compatibility: Anything that won't eat it

Tank size: 10 gallons

Temperament: Peaceful

Price range: $10-$40

Life span: 3-5 years

Buying tips: They should be in a group at the bottom of the tank.

Camel Shrimp

Fishpedia Saltwater

Shrimp, Harlequin

Common name: Harlequin Shrimp

Scientific name: *Hymenoceridae*

Habitat: Reefs

Size: 2-3"

Diet: Carnivore, live starfish feet

Parameters: 8 pH

Compatibility: Anything that won't eat them

Tank size: 10 gallons

Temperament: Peaceful

Price range: $15-$45

Life span: 5-7 years

Buying tips: They should be white with purple/light pink spots.

Harlequin Shrimp

Fishpedia **Saltwater**

Shrimp, Peppermint

Common name: Peppermint Shrimp

Scientific name: *Hippolytidae*

Habitat: Reefs

Size: 1-2"

Diet: Omnivore

Parameters: 8 pH

Compatibility: Fish too small to eat it

Tank size: 10 gallons

Temperament: Peaceful

Price range: $10-$20

Life span: 2 years

Buying tips: It should be foraging around the walls/sand.

Peppermint Shrimp

Fishpedia **Saltwater**

Snail, Bumblebee

Common name: Bumblebee Snail / Margarita Snail / Nerite Snail

Scientific name: *Pisaniidae*

Habitat: Reefs

Size: 1-3"

Diet: Herbivore

Parameters: 8 pH

Compatibility: Anything that doesn't eat snails

Tank size: 10 gallons

Temperament: Peaceful

Price range: $2-$10

Life span: 1-2 years

Buying tips: They should have no cracks in their shells.

Bumblebee Snail

Fishpedia **Saltwater**

Starfish, Brittle

Common name: Brittle Starfish

Scientific name: *Ophiocomidae*

Habitat: Reefs

Size: 4-20"

Diet: Omnivore

Parameters: 8 pH

Compatibility: Anything that won't eat it

Tank size: 20 gallons

Temperament: Peaceful

Price range: $10-$20

Life span: 5 years

Buying tips: They should have all of their limbs.

Brittle Starfish

Fishpedia Saltwater

Tangs

Common name: Tangs

Scientific name: *Acanthuridae*

Habitat: Reefs

Size: 5-12"

Diet: Herbivore

Parameters: 8 pH

Compatibility: Medium-sized, peaceful fish

Tank size: 75-350 gallons

Temperament: Peaceful

Price range: $40-$1,000

Life span: 15-20 years

Buying tips: They should be moving non-stop through rocks.

Tangs

Fishpedia **Saltwater**

Urchin, Tuxedo

Common name: Tuxedo Urchin

Scientific name: *Temnopleuridae*

Habitat: Reefs

Size: 2-3"

Diet: Omnivore

Parameters: 8 pH

Compatibility: Anything that doesn't eat sea urchins

Tank size: 30 gallons

Temperament: Peaceful

Price range: $10-$30

Life span: 2-5 years

Buying tips: There should be no spines on the bottom of the tank.

Tuxedo Urchin

Acknowledgements

There are a number of people who were very important during the process of researching and writing this book. I would like to acknowledge a number of them: Sophia, who put up with my endless chatter about fish; Dad, who drove me to the fish store countless times; Mom and "The Grabber" (my crayfish) for inspiring me to write this book; everybody on the online forums and the Wet Pets crew who have helped me so much on this journey; my editor, Allison, for taking me as seriously as any other author and for editing this book; and my teacher, Ms. Otwell, for helping me so much during the early stages.

Well, that's all for this book. Keep a look out for the next ;). While this book contains everything you need to get started, there's plenty more to learn. On my website, fishkeepingforkids.com, I have a blog and a couple websites linked to go and check out, as well as some good books and magazines to read Keep in mind this is more of a guide than a specific how-to, for every fishkeeper has a slightly different perspective on the ethics of fishkeeping (such as the minimum tank size to keep a fish "happy"), as well as the maximum size of fish and the minimum tank size. Developing your own view of fishkeeping can be one of the best parts of the hobby. If you are interested in continuing fishkeeping as a hobby, there are many next steps, but those are for a future book. I hope you have a fascinating journey through fishkeeping with this book as your guide!

-Brian

Image Attributions

1   Planted tank with tetras

https://www.aquasabi.com/aquascaping-wiki_fish_tetras-in-a-planted-tank

2   Big saltwater tank with coral

https://reefbuilders.com/2016/03/14/the-coral-packed-reef-tank-of-aquatic-art-inc/

3   Chart of the nitrogen cycle

https://modestfish.com/how-to-cycle-your-aquarium/

4   Types of filters

https://www.yihufish.com/fishkeeping-articles/freshwater/my-first-freshwater-aquarium/types-of-filters/

5   Empty glass tank

https://www.amazon.com/Aquarium-Tank-Glass-5-1-Gal/dp/B005VDO7QO

6   Chart of the different lights

https://www.tropicalfishsite.com/the-pros-and-cons-of-different-aquarium-fish-tank-lighting-sources/

7   Photo of a heater

https://aquariumsphere.com/aquarium-heater-broken/

8   Large chart of the fish diseases

http://boeing_dude.tripod.com/id31.htm

9   Quarantine tank

https://www.reddit.com/r/bettafish/comments/66m30z/for_anyone_following_this_is_my_setup_and/

10   Picture of fish medicine

https://www.seachem.com/kanaplex.php

11   Dead fish

http://www.aquariumfiltersetup.com/common-aquarium-problems/dead-fish/

12   Ember tetras

https://tankaddict.com/ember-tetra/

13   Congo tetras

https://www.aquariumsource.com/congo-tetra/

14   Bloodfin tetras

https://azgardens.com/product/glass-bloodfin-tropical-tetra/

15   Glowlight tetras

https://www.liveaquaria.com/product/1583/?pcatid=1583

16   Cardinal tetras
https://wattleydiscus.com/product/cardinal-tetras/

17   Neon tetras
https://theifishstore.com/products/neon-tetra

18   Guppies
https://www.aquariumcoop.com/blogs/aquarium/guppy-care-guide

19   Oscar
https://www.thesprucepets.com/oscar-fish-species-profile-5079536

20   Mollies
https://aquascaper.org/the-algae-eating-fish-for-aquarium-mollies

21   Platies
https://www.aquariumcoop.com/blogs/aquarium/platy-care-guide

22   Swordtails
https://www.aquariumnexus.com/swordtail-fish-water-temperature/

23   Cherry barbs
https://azgardens.com/product/cherry-barb-tropical-fish/

24   Tiger barbs
https://aquariumtidings.com/tiger-barb-fish/

25   Tinfoil barbs
https://www.petesaquariums.com/shop/tropical-aquarium-fish/red-tail-tinfoil-barb/

26   Rosy barbs
https://aquadiction.world/species-spotlight/rosy-barb/

27   Golden dwarf barbs
https://bluegrassaquatics.com/dwarf-golden-barb-regular.html

28   Ruby barbs
https://azgardens.com/product/black-ruby-barb-tropical-fish/

29   Dwarf gourami
https://www.fishkeepingworld.com/dwarf-gourami/

30   Honey gourami
https://aquadiction.world/species-spotlight/honey-gourami/

31   Pearl gourami
https://www.amazon.com/Pearl-Gourami-Inches-Freshwater-Tropical/dp/B074CRD1RQ

32   Moonlight gourami
https://aquadiction.world/species-spotlight/moonlight-gourami/

33   Betta
https://www.livescience.com/betta-fish.html

34   Norman's Lampeye killifish
https://aquaticarts.com/products/normans-lampeye-killifish

35   Clown loach
https://www.fishkeepingworld.com/clown-loach/

36   Yo-yo loach
https://aquadiction.world/species-spotlight/yoyo-loach/

37   Weather loach
https://www.loaches.com/species-index/weather-loach-misgurnis-anguillicaudatus

38   Freshwater angelfish
https://www.ratemyfishtank.com/blog/everything-you-need-to-know-about-freshwater-angelfish

39   Dwarf corydoras
https://www.practicalfishkeeping.co.uk/features/the-littlest-hobos/

40   Bronze corydoras
https://www.encyclo-fish.com/EN/freshwater/fishes/corydoras-aeneus.php

41   Pygmy angelfish
https://www.tankfacts.com/fish/saltwater/angel-dwarf/pygmy-angelfish_872

42   Flame angelfish
https://www.liveaquaria.com/product/444/?pcatid=444

43   Coral beauty angelfish
https://www.algaebarn.com/blog/captive-bred-fish/angelfish/coral-beauty-angelfish-the-best-first-angel/

44   Potter's angelfish
https://www.waikikiaquarium.org/experience/animal-guide/fishes/angelfishes/potters-angelfish/

45   Midnight angelfish
https://www.aquariumdomain.com/SpeciesProfiles/MarineFish/MidnightAngelfish.shtml

46   Flameback angelfish
https://reefbuilders.com/2018/05/25/african-flameback-angelfish-centropyge-acanthops/

47   Rock beauty angelfish
https://www.liveaquaria.com/product/423/?pcatid=423

48   Firefish
https://www.google.com/url?q=https://www.thesprucepets.com/firefish-goby-nemateleotris-magnifica-2924294&sa=D&source=editors&ust=1616617698130000&usg=AFQjCNFfMQhxJ2b9_MW8fFq5vVc3fUq_gA

49   Purple firefish
https://www.google.com/url?q=https://reefbuilders.com/2014/01/29/purple-firefish-dartfish-nemateleotris-decora-shy-small-peaceful/&sa=D&source=editors&ust=1616617906323000&usg=AFQjCNF02NmNEGOeDNh9gQcQeBthihSSEQ

50   Helfrichi firefish
https://www.nano-reef.com/forums/topic/216472-helfrichi-firefish/

51   Unicorn tang
https://www.britannica.com/animal/unicorn-fish-Naso-genus

52   Blue tang
https://www.saltwaterfish.com/product-blue-hippo-tang-medium

53   Yellow tang
https://vividaquariums.com/products/yellow-tang

54   Flame fin tomini tang
https://forums.saltwaterfish.com/threads/center-piece-fish-ideas.392440/

55   Yellowhead jawfish
https://www.kpaquatics.com/product/yellowhead-jawfish/

56   Chinstrap jawfish
https://reefbuilders.com/2014/02/07/opistognathus-sp-6-chinstrap-jawfish-amusing-fish/

57   Blue dot jawfish
https://reefs.com/fish/blue-spotted-jawfish/

58   Black cap jawfish
https://www.liveaquaria.com/product/182/?pcatid=182

59   Flame goby
https://flabbywhalefish.com/2017/01/24/species-profile-flaming-prawn-goby/

60   Greenbanded goby
https://flabbywhalefish.com/2017/01/24/species-profile-flaming-prawn-goby/

61   Yasha shrimp goby
https://www.melevsreef.com/critter/yasha-goby

62   Maroon clownfish
https://www.saltwaterfishshop.com/product/maroon-clownfish-for-sale/

63   Percula clownfish
https://vividaquariums.com/products/percula-clownfish

64   Green chromis
https://www.petesaquariums.com/shop/saltwater-aquarium-fish/damselfish/green-chromis-damselfish-or-blue-green-chromis/

65   Azure damselfish
https://www.tankfacts.com/fish/saltwater/damsel/azure-damselfish_463

66   Sunset anthias
https://www.aquariumdomain.com/SpeciesProfiles/MarineFish/SunsetAnthias.shtml

67   Sunburst anthias
https://reefbuilders.com/2014/01/13/awesome-fish-spotlight-serranocirrhitus-latus-sunburst-anthias/

68   Squareback anthias
https://www.marinefishez.com/saltwater-fish/anthias/male-square-anthias-detail

69   Fuzzy dwarf lionfish
https://www.reddit.com/r/Aquariums/comments/6x4onj/my_baby_fuzzy_dwarf_lionfish_cocoa/

70   Volitan lionfish
https://www.marinefishez.com/saltwater-fish/lionfish/black-volitan-lionfish-detail

71   Marine betta
http://www.discountaquariumsaz.com/fish-store-aquarium-store-fish-shop-fish-tank-store/marine-betta-fish/

72   Valentini pufferfish
https://www.saltwaterfish.com/product-valentini-puffer

73   Porcupine pufferfish
https://www.saltwaterfish.com/product-porcupine-puffer

74   Cherry shrimp
https://somethingfishydbq.com/product/cherry-shrimp/

75   Snowball shrimp
https://trinsfish.com/5-snowball-shrimp/

76   Red crystal shrimp
https://aquariumtidings.com/red-crystal-shrimp-care/

77   Amano shrimp
https://www.garnelenhaus.com/garnelenhaus/amano-shrimp

78   Panther crab
https://azgardens.com/product/panther-crabs/

79   Thai micro crab
https://www.reddit.com/r/Aquariums/comments/epefa6/thai_micro_crab_smallest_known_fully_aquatic/

80   White crayfish
https://www.aquariumcarebasics.com/aquarium-crayfish/white-crayfish/

81   Mystery snail
https://www.aquariumsource.com/mystery-snail/

82   Freshwater nerite snail
https://www.aquariumcarebasics.com/freshwater-snails/nerite-snails/

83   Peppermint shrimp
https://quantumreefs.com/products/peppermint-shrimp-lysmata-wurdemanni-complex

84   Brittle starfish
https://www.thefishkeeper.co.za/brittle-stars-in-the-aquarium/

85   Emerald crab
https://www.reef2reef.com/threads/reef-aquarium-fact-325-not-all-emerald-crabs-will-eat-bubble-algae.123546/

86   Tuxedo urchin
https://quantumreefs.com/products/blue-tuxedo-urchin-mespilia-globulus

87   Debelius's reef lobster
https://www.aquariumdomain.com/SpeciesProfiles/MarineInverts/DebeliusReefLobster.shtml

88   Arrow crab
https://www.aquariadise.com/arrow-crab/

89   Halloween hermit crab
https://aquariumbreeder.com/halloween-hermit-crab-detailed-guide-care-diet-and-breeding/

90   Scarlet reef hermit crab
https://www.tankfacts.com/invertebrates/saltwater/crab/scarlet-reef-hermit-crab_30

91   Condy anemone
https://reefs.com/2018/04/14/the-severe-health-risk-posed-by-the-caribbean-condylactis-anemone/

92   Lettuce sea slug
https://www.whatsthatfish.com/fish/lettuce-sea-slug/1581

93   Bumblebee snail
https://www.aquariumfishsale.com/products/bumblebee-snail

94   Marine nerite snail
https://www.melevsreef.com/critter/nerite-snail

95   Margarita snail
https://www.aquariumfishsale.com/products/black-margarita-snail

96   Bala shark
https://www.fishkeepingworld.com/bala-shark/

97   Goldfish
https://www.tfhmagazine.com/articles/freshwater/goldfish-myths-debunked

98   Pleco
https://be.chewy.com/avoid-the-pleco-predicament/

99   Clown knifefish
https://www.worldwidefishandpets.com/product/6-to7-clown-knifefish/

100   Zebra macana knifefish
https://www.seriouslyfish.com/species/gymnotus-pedanopterus/

101   Black ghost knifefish
https://www.aquariadise.com/black-ghost-knifefish/

102   Apple snail
https://en.wikipedia.org/wiki/Ampullariidae

103   Panther grouper
https://www.thefishkeeper.co.za/the-panther-grouper/

104   Java fern
https://www.liveaquaria.com/product/800/?pcatid=800

105   Java moss
https://www.thesprucepets.com/java-moss-1381198

106   Amazon sword plant
https://www.liveaquaria.com/product/802/?pcatid=802

107   Chrysantha
https://www.liveaquaria.com/product/788/?pcatid=788

108   Banana plant
https://fishlab.com/aquarium-banana-plant/

109   Anubias nana
https://www.liveaquaria.com/product/815/?pcatid=815

110   Water wisteria
https://www.tokyuaquatic.com/products/water-wisteria-hygrophila-difformis-live-aquarium-plants-freshwater-decorations

111   Marimo moss ball
https://www.amazon.com/Aquatic-Arts-Marimo-Moss-Balls/dp/B01BKW59KC

112   Clump of Java moss
https://www.ebay.com/itm/DIY-Java-Moss-and-Holder-Live-Aquarium-Biological-Ball-Moss-Holder-K3K2-/164358204905

113   Blue mandarin
https://www.australiangeographic.com.au/blogs/creatura-blog/2015/05/beware-of-the-beautiful-but-poisonous-mandarinfish/

114   Atlantic pygmy octopus
https://octolab.tv/species/atlantic-pygmy-octopus/

115   Tiger tail sea cucumber
https://vividaquariums.com/products/tiger-tail-cucumber

116   Spiny sea cucumber
https://vividaquariums.com/products/spiny-sea-cucumber

117   Indian vagabond butterflyfish
https://www.saltwaterfish.com/product-indian-vagabond-butterfly

118   Snowflake eel
https://www.reefs4less.com/product/snowflake-eel/

119   Banded pipefish
https://reefs.com/fish/banded-pipefish/

120   Bluestripe pipefish
https://www.petfishforsale.com/blue-stripe-pipefish/

121   Dwarf seahorse
https://www.liveaquaria.com/product/283/?pcatid=283

122   Camel shrimp
https://www.marinefishez.com/inverts-mmore/shrimp/camel-shrimp-detail

123　Peppermint angelfish
https://www.liveaquaria.com/general/general.cfm?general_pagesid=629

124　Platinum arowana
https://arowanafishforsale.com/product/platinum-arowana/

125　Harlequin shrimp
https://seaunseen.com/harlequin-shrimp-2/

126　Hardware
http://www.aquariumfiltersetup.com/aquarium-essentials/aquarium-rocks/

127　Software
https://aquariumplants.com/12-plant-assortment-hardy-low-light/

128　Pea pufferfish
https://www.tfhmagazine.com/articles/freshwater/the-dwarf-puffer-a-pleasant-little-surprise

129　Oto catfish
https://www.aquariumcarebasics.com/freshwater-aquarium-fish/otocinclus-catfish/

130　Ropefish
https://thebrackishtank.tumblr.com/post/95231309294/ropefish-reedfish-genus-erpetoichthys-species

131　Tire-track eel
https://azgardens.com/product/spiny-tire-track-eel/

132　Red devil cichlid
https://www.ebay.com/itm/Red-Devil-Cichlid-2-/284169498730

133　Peacock cichlids
https://theifishstore.com/products/yellow-sunshine-peacock

134　Lyretail anthias
https://coralsfishandbeyond.com/products/red-lyretail-anthias-pseudanthias-cheirospilos

135　Squaretail bristletooth tang
https://www.tankfacts.com/fish/saltwater/tang-and-surgeons/squaretail-bristletooth-tang_598

136　Fish eating
https://www.fishkeepingworld.com/what-do-fish-eat/

137　Flake food
https://www.amazon.com/Tropical-Flakes-Aquatic-Foods-Premium/dp/B01BFOM7AU

138　Baby brine shrimp
https://www.thesprucepets.com/diy-hatching-brine-shrimp-2924618

139   Frozen bloodworm cube

https://www.facebook.com/PetCityPhilippines/posts/frozen-bloodworm-24-cubes-per-padavailable-pet-city-cartimar-pasay-branchcontact/2744075125611275/

140   Siphon

https://aquariumhall.com/siphon-pump-in-fish-tank/

141   Wet Pets

https://www.facebook.com/wetpetsbysteve/

142   Flip aquatics

https://flipaquatics.com/

143   Freshwater compatibility chart

https://docs.google.com/spreadsheets/d/1e2AuieS66V_AObc3E9wEt347vVlTooFhygPStq4HkXo/edit#gid=0

144   Aquarium with sick fish

https://smartaquariumguide.com/freshwater-fish-diseases-symptoms-remedies/

145   Dying aquatic plant

https://www.myaquariumclub.com/leafy-plants-dying-or-something-in-fry-tank-554365.html

146   Fish acclimating

https://kenyamarinecenter.com/the-right-way-to-acclimate-incoming-fish/

References

"Perfect Pea Puffer: Is This Cute Dwarf Fish Ideal For Your Tank?" *Fishkeeping World*. www.fishkeepingworld.com. https://www.fishkeepingworld.com/pea-puffer/

"Miniatus Grouper and Volitan Lionfish." *The Marine Compatibility Guide*. http://www.marinecompatibilityguide.com/ http://www.marinecompatibilityguide.com/miniatusgrouper/volitanlionfish

"Black Ghost Knifefish Care Guide – Tank Requirements, Diet, Breeding and Much More." *Fisharoma*. www.fisharoma.com. https://fisharoma.com/black-ghost-knifefish/

"Cockatoo Cichlid Information | Aquatic Mag." *Pinterest*. www.pinterest.com. https://www.pinterest.com/pin/227431849912668786/

"What Is the Nitrogen Cycling Process in a Saltwater Aquarium?" *The Spruce Pets*. www.thesprucepets.com. https://www.thesprucepets.com/what-is-the-nitrogen-cycling-process-2924241

"June26.com." *Pinterest*. www.pinterest.com. https://www.pinterest.com/pin/108649409743761556/

"How to Set up a Planted Aquarium: The Complete Step-By-Step Guide." *BYA*. www.buildyouraquarium.com. https://www.buildyouraquarium.com/setting-up-planted-aquarium/

"Golden Dwarf Barb (Pethia Gelius)." *fahad's blog*. http://www.fahadismy.name/. Accessed November 6, 2019.

"Unicorn Tang." *Aquarium Solutions Cambodia*. www.aquarium-solutions-cambodia.com. Accessed November 25, 2019 https://www.aquarium-solutions-cambodia.com/product-page/unicorn-tang-6-10-cm*

"Greenbanded Goby." *Aquariumdomain.com* www.aquariumdomain.com. Accessed April 18, 2020 https://www.aquariumdomain.com/adSocial/index.php/greenbanded-goby/*

"The First Ever Aquacultured Yasha Gobies Announced." *Aqua Nerd*. aquanerd.com/2016/07/the-first-ever-aquacultured-yasha-gobies-announced.html. Accessed April 21, 2020 https://aquanerd.com/2016/07/the-first-ever-aquacultured-yasha-gobies-announced.html*

"Square Anthias Male." *MarineFishEZ.* www.marinefishez.com/saltwater-fish/anthias/male-square-anthias-detail. Accessed April 21, 2020 https://www.marinefishez.com/saltwater-fish/anthias/male-square-anthias-detail*

"Caresheet: Thai micro crab | Limnopilos naiyanetri." *Aquariadise.* www.aquariadise.com/caresheet-thai-micro-crab-limnopilos-naiyanetri/. Accessed April 24, 2020 https://www.aquariadise.com/caresheet-thai-micro-crab-limnopilos-naiyanetri/*

"Java Fern." *Liveaquaria.* www.liveaquaria.com/product/800/?pcatid=800. Accessed May 7, 2020 https://www.liveaquaria.com/product/800/?pcatid=800

"Java Moss On A Bamboo Stick." *Liveaquaria.* www.liveaquaria.com/product/prod_display.cfm?c=768+1632+7115&pcatid=7115. Accessed May 7, 2020 https://www.liveaquaria.com/product/prod_display.cfm?c=768+1632+7115&pcatid=7115

"Amazon Sword Plant." *Liveaquaria.* www.liveaquaria.com/product/prod_display.cfm?c=768+1632+802&pcatid=802. Accessed May 7, 2020 https://www.liveaquaria.com/product/prod_display.cfm?c=768+1632+802&pcatid=802*

"Chrysantha." *Liveaquaria.* www.liveaquaria.com/product/788/chrysantha?pcatid=788&c=900+771+788. Accessed May 7, 2020 https://www.liveaquaria.com/product/788/chrysantha?pcatid=788&c=900+771+788*

 "Banana Plant." *Liveaquaria.* www.liveaquaria.com/product/prod_display.cfm?c=768+1630+791&pcatid=791. Accessed May 7, 2020 https://www.liveaquaria.com/product/prod_display.cfm?c=768+1630+791&pcatid=791

"Anubias Nana." *Liveaquaria.* www.liveaquaria.com/product/prod_display.cfm?c=768+1630+815&pcatid=815. Accessed May 7, 2020 https://www.liveaquaria.com/product/prod_display.cfm?c=768+1630+815&pcatid=815

"Wisteria." *Liveaquaria.* www.liveaquaria.com/product/prod_display.cfm?c=768+1632+824&pcatid=824. Accessed May 7, 2020 https://www.liveaquaria.com/product/prod_display.cfm?c=768+1632+824&pcatid=824*

"Harlequin Shrimp." *Liveaquaria.* www.liveaquaria.com/product/prod_display.cfm?c=497+525+749&pcatid=749. Accessed May 7, 2020 https://www.liveaquaria.com/product/prod_display.cfm?c=497+525+749&pcatid=749*

"The Sturdy but Shy Marine Betta." *Saltwater Smarts*. www.saltwatersmarts.com/marine-betta-calloplesiops-altivelis-argus-shy-3640/. Accessed May 14, 2020 https://www.saltwatersmarts.com/marine-betta-calloplesiops-altivelis-argus-shy-3640/

"Snowball shrimp – Detailed Guide: Care, Diet and Breeding." *Aquarium Breeder*. aquariumbreeder.com/snowball-shrimp-detailed-guide-care-diet-and-breeding/. Accessed May 14, 2020 https://aquariumbreeder.com/snowball-shrimp-detailed-guide-care-diet-and-breeding/

Martin, Mark W., and Ret Talbot. 2009. The complete idiot's guide to saltwater aquariums. New York, N.Y.: Alpha

Index

M

N

O

P

About the Author

Brian Conway enjoys fishkeeping, homeschooling, soccer and fishing. One of his favorite places to be is the local aquarium, the Oklahoma Aquarium. When he first started on the fishkeeping journey, all of the available books were either too basic to give him any new information or too advanced for him to understand. Fishkeeping for Kids started as an assignment for homeschooling, but Brian decided he would publish it to help solve this problem for others. Fishkeeping for Kids is Brian's first book, but he enjoyed writing the first so much, he is already working on his next. He currently lives in Oklahoma with his parents, younger sister and four-legged friend Asia. You can follow him online at fishkeepingforkids.com.

www.ingramcontent.com/pod-product-compliance
Lightning Source LLC
Chambersburg PA
CBHW041214030426
42336CB00023B/3344